Teaching
Gifted Children

Teaching
Gifted Children

Owenita Sanderlin

South Brunswick and New York: A. S. Barnes and Company
London: Thomas Yoseloff Ltd

A. S. Barnes and Co., Inc.
Cranbury, New Jersey 08512

Thomas Yoseloff Ltd
108 New Bond Street
London W1Y OQX, England

Library of Congress Cataloging in Publication Data

Sanderlin, Owenita.
    Teaching gifted children.

    Bibliography: p.
    1. Gifted children—Education. I. Title.
LC3993.S24   371.9′53   72-6375
ISBN 0-498-01160-7

Printed in the United States of America

to

Cecil Munsey and David Hermanson

for all their help
and kindness

Contents

Acknowledgments

The author gratefully acknowledges the generous assistance and encouragement of Dr. David P. Hermanson, Coordinator of the Secondary Gifted Programs of the San Diego City Schools, and District Resource Teacher Cecil Munsey, who opened doors to inexhaustible resources, both human and documentary.

Chief among these were Dr. Richmond Barbour, Assistant Superintendent of Schools, Student Services Division, who has been a leader in gifted education in San Diego for many years; Dr. David C. Wright, Director of Exceptional Child Services, whose doctoral dissertation (with Dr. Hermanson) appraised the "school within a school," one of the most interesting gifted programs I know of; Mrs. Evelyn Curry, Coordinator of Elementary Gifted Programs and Ole Kittelson, District Resource Teacher; Lois Bailey, psychologist in the Pupil Study Center; Patty Bruner and Marilyn Post, "gifted" secretaries; Florence Stephens, librarian in the professional library at the San Diego Education Center; Marian Williams, President of San Diego Educators of the Gifted (teachers) and Beth Smith, President of San Diego Association for Gifted Children (parents); Joene Bruhn, counselor in charge of gifted programs at Hale Junior High, T. A. Stormy Weathers and their students; Dr. Larry Meyers and Charlotte Malone, teachers of gifted teachers; Michael Lorch and C. K. Fristrom, Robert Haas, Jim Grove, Betty Morrison, Dr. Melvin Zeddies and all their "independent" students who, along with my own children, provided much human interest. I am also indebted to many other teachers and students, including especially Mary Jane Cyga's classes at Einstein, Arnold Boucher's and Ted Muradian's, at Gage Elementary and Collier Junior High; and to Don Giddings, Principal, and Mrs. Opal DiMatteo of Patrick Henry High.

Dr. Hermanson also made it possible for me to meet such

national leaders as Professor John Curtis Gowan, President of the National Association for Gifted Children and of The Association for Gifted division of the Council for Exceptional Children, a consultant for gifted programs, professor at San Fernando Valley State College and author of many books on gifted education; Dr. William Vassar, Consultant for Gifted Programs in Connecticut, who was instrumental in promoting the recent national survey disclosing the "widespread neglect" of the gifted, and who is currently working on national legislation designed to improve these conditions; June Shartzer, Consultant in the outstanding Illinois Gifted Programs; Dr. Gerald Stanley, Coordinator of the well-known gifted programs in Garden Grove, California; and Mrs. Ruthe Lundy, Coordinator, Palo Alto, California, which is noted for its innovative model programs that often utilize the facilities of Stanford University.

For the photographs, the author wishes to thank Professor E. Paul Torrance of the University of Georgia for a number of illustrations of creativity in education; Cecil Munsey; Mary Ann Cyga; Dr. William Vassar and DeWitt Zuse, Director of the Educational Center for the Arts, in Connecticut; Mrs. Evelyn Curry; Mrs. Joene Bruhn and Stormy Weathers; Dr. and Mrs. E. R. Simmons of the Gifted Students Foundation, Dallas, Texas; June Shartzer of Illinois, Dr. Lawrence Meyers of Temple Beth Israel School; Mrs. Ruthe Lundy; Melvin Zeddes, Ned Wilson and the students in the Independent Study Center at Morse High School in San Diego; Sibyl Eickner and Dorothy Mason, teachers in the gifted typing program; and Betty Jensen of John Marshall High School, Portland, Oregon.

And finally, for the "controversy" at the beginnings of the chapters, the author is indebted to the following authors and publishers:

Allyn and Bacon, Inc. for permission to use the short passages from J. Richard Suchman's speech "Inquiry and Education" printed in James J. Gallagher, *Teaching Gifted Students.*

Editors of *The Atlantic Monthly* for permission to quote material from their introduction to Richard Herrnstein's "I. Q."

Center for Applied Research, 70 Fifth Ave., New York City 10011 for permission to quote material from Robert F. DeHaan, *Accelerated Learning Programs.*

James Bryant Conant, for his permission to quote material from his book *The Comprehensive High School.*

Delacorte Press for permission to quote material from George B. Leonard, *Education and Ecstasy* and from Neil Postman, *Teaching as a Subversive Activity.*

E. P. Dutton and Co., Inc. for permission to quote material from John Holt, *What do I Do Monday?;* Evelyn Sharp, *Thinking Is Child's Play;* Ruth Strang, *Helping Your Gifted Child.*

Gifted Child Quarterly and Ann F. Isaacs, John Curtis Gowan, E. Paul Torrance and J. P. Guilford for their permission to quote from various articles printed in the magazine.

Mr. Benjamin H. Florence, Executor of the Estate of Henry L. Hollingworth for his permission to quote from material that originally appeared in *Children Above 180 IQ,* by Leta Hollingworth, published by Harcourt Brace Jovanovich, Inc.

Harper and Row, Publishers, Inc. for permission to quote material from Willard Abraham, *Common Sense about Gifted Children;* Maya Pines, *Revolution in Learning;* John Gardner, *Excellence;* Alvin Eurich, *Reforming American Education;* Louise Bates Ames, *Is Your Child in the Wrong Grade?*

Harvard Educational Review for permission to reprint three brief extracts from the magazine, written by Arthur R. Jensen.

Harvard University Press for permission to quote material from Jerome S. Bruner, *The Process of Education.*

Mr. John S. Hollister, Project Administrator, Conant Studies of American Education, for permission to quote material from James B. Conant, *The American High School Today.*

Liveright Publishers, New York, for permission to quote from Bertrand Russell, *Education and the Good Life.* Copyright ® 1954 by Bertrand Russell.

The Macmillan Company for permission to quote from Benjamin Fine, *Your Child and School* (Copyright © Benjamin Fine 1965);

To Random House and Alfred A. Knopf Inc. for permission to quote from George Thomas and Joseph Crescimbeni, *Guiding the Gifted Child,* © 1966 by Random House, Inc.; Charles E. Silberman, *Crisis in the Classroom,* © 1970 by Charles E. Silberman; Gilbert Highet, *The Art of Teaching,* copyright © 1950 by Gilbert Highet.

Saturday Review for permission to quote from Ivan Illich "The Alternative to Schooling," which appeared in the June 19, 1971 issue (copyright © 1971, Saturday Review, Inc.); Benjamin De-Mott's review of *How to Survive in Your Native Land,* by James Herndon, which appeared in the September 18, 1971 issue (copyright © 1971 by Saturday Review, Inc.); John I. Goodlad, "Meeting Children Where They Are," which appeared in the March 10, 1965, issue (copyright © 1965 by Saturday Review, Inc.); John I. Goodlad, "The Schools vs. Education," which appeared in the April 19, 1969 issue (copyright © 1969 by Saturday Review, Inc.).

Schocken Books Inc. for permission to quote from Maria Montessori, *Spontaneous Activity in Education, Dr. Montessori's Own Handbook* and *The Montessori Method.*

Simon and Schuster Inc. for permission to quote from James Herndon, *The Way It Spozed To Be* (copyright © 1965, 1968 by James Herndon); Siegfried and Therese Engelmann, *Give Your Child a Superior Mind* (copyright © 1966 by Siegfried and Therese Engelmann; Daniel Boorstin, *The Sociology of the Absurd,* copyright © 1969, 1970 by Daniel J. Boorstin; Joan Beck, *How To Raise a Brighter Child,* copyright © 1967 by Joan Beck.

Stanford University Press for permission to quote from Lewis Terman and Melita Oden, *The Gifted Child Grows Up, Genetic Studies of Genius* Volume IV, pp. 18, 14, 9, 281, and 264 (the order in which they are cited in the book).

Charles C. Thomas, Publisher, for permission to quote material from John Curtis Gowan and George D. Demos, *The Education and Guidance of the Ablest.* Courtesy of Charles C. Thomas, Publisher, Springfield, Illinois.

An Introduction to the Controversy

Can parents or teachers develop more gifted children through infant and early childhood education? Should children start school before five?

Is education for the gifted undemocratic?

Who are the gifted? What is an IQ? How valid is it? Can it be changed? Is the IQ concept of giftedness outmoded?

Is intelligence chiefly hereditary? How much can it be affected by environment?

Are children of superior intelligence likely to be emotionally disturbed? Physically weak? Unsociable?

Are bright children bored in our schools?

What can parents do? How much say should they have in their own children's education?

Should children be grouped by age? Ability? Some other way?

Should children who are capable of learning faster be accelerated in school? If so, how? What about enrichment?

How should gifted children be taught? What makes a good "gifted" teacher?

What are the chances of making any changes in our countrywide lockstep system of education? What should they be?

How much can we afford to do for the gifted? Where do we get the money? Can better education for the gifted lead to improvements in the education of all children?

These questions have been asked for so many generations that we wonder if they'll ever be answered, although at the present moment there is a new hope—lately the word *dream* has come into respectable use—that they will.

In 1848, educators imported a "pilot project," based on the German graded school, into the United States. A special building was erected to house the first one, the three-story Quincey Grammar School in Boston, Massachusetts, with twelve rooms of equal size, one teacher and up to 55 pupils who stayed in each room for a school year.

The enthusiastic educational innovators predicted that this system would be the pattern for education for 50 years; as we all know, that estimate was conservative. Practically everything else has changed, but not the average American school. Whether we are college students taking education courses in order to teach, new or older teachers or administrators, parents or grandparents, we have been to such schools, and most of our children still sit in similar rooms.

Even though over seventy years ago, President Charles W. Eliot of Harvard said the stereotyped patterns of a graded school system demand a stereotyped individual as learner; even though in 1912 Frederick Burk, President of San Francisco State Normal School, published a book about individualized instruction, called *Remedy for Lockstep Schooling,* our children are still shackled by lockstep methods of education. Everyone admits students don't learn at the same pace, that slow learners are "passed" along from grade to grade in increasing bewilderment, and faster learners are held back to waste hours of their lives in drills and reviews of material they have already mastered. Even the "average" student (who doesn't exist) may be a whiz at arithmetic before he can read, or a reader who needs more help in math; but he gets the standard amount of teacher-time in both. Granted, not all schools are like this now. There's a light at the end of the tunnel; new ways *are* being tried.

Since architecture, as demonstrated by the Quincey Grammar School, can have much to do with education, the bright new "open" schools which are being built here and there today may well be the forerunners (as well as the result) of a more open kind of education. Many people have never seen such a school, even though there may be one or two in their own districts. Whether near or far, every parent, teacher, school board member or administrator should make it a point to visit one. What we don't see, we don't understand—or, in the case of these colorful, comfortable new schools—are not tempted by. We should also visit new programs in older schools, such as the NASSP's Model Schools Project[1] or teacher-initiated pilot programs in innovative school districts.

In the 1770s, Americans pioneered a new freedom in government; in the 1970s, leaders are pioneering a new freedom in education. Gifted teachers, administrators and students will have much to do with the success of the necessary experimentation that must precede any worthwhile change. Throughout history, the creative thinkers, the gifted leaders have been the pioneers, not only because of their physical courage but because they have the intellectual courage to try something that has never been done before.

We don't have all the answers yet, certainly, and before we can make any widespread changes we have to listen to the debate. Unfortunately, no matter how exciting and successful a new kind of schooling turns out to be, it can be—and too often is—buried under an avalanche of uninformed community criticism. The average citizen doesn't want to try anything new until it has been proved, yet how can it be proved until it's tested?

"We have not retreated," Don Giddings, principal of innovative Patrick Henry High, told me recently, "but we have retrenched, in order to get the community behind us. *And we have.*"

Too often, promising programs have to be abandoned after a successful year or two because only a few enthusiastic students and teachers know what's going on. The money runs out, parents get worried, and there goes the financial and moral support they *must* have, and probably would have, if people just knew more about it.

So let's begin by discussing those questions everybody asks, and then go on to describe some of the programs: what can be done for our best students, why it should be done, and how it will help all students, everywhere.

---

1. See J. Lloyd Trump and William Georgiades, "Doing Better With What You Have, NASSP Model Schools Project," *The Bulletin, National Association of Secondary School Principals,* 54, no. 346 (May 1970). An off-print is available from NASSP.

Teaching
Gifted Children

1
What about Early Childhood Education?

PLATO (about 2400 years ago): *The most important part of education is right training in the nursery.* (*Laws,* 643).

MARIA MONTESSORI (Italian foundress of the Montessori Method of early childhood education popular in modern advanced preschools, 1917): *Woe to us, when we believe ourselves responsible for matters that do not concern us, and delude ourselves with the idea that we are perfecting things that will perfect themselves quite independently of us. . . . What a relief to say: "Nature will take care of that. I will leave my baby free, and watch him grow in beauty; I will be a quiescent spectator of the miracle."*[1]

MAYA PINES (writer-reporter, under a Carnegie grant, 1966): *Millions of children are being irreparably damaged by our failure to stimulate them intellectually during their crucial years—birth to six.*

FITZHUGH DODSON (psychologist, educator, founder of La Primera Preschool, consultant Head Start, 1970): *. . . the more intellectual stimulation you can give your child in the first five years of his life,* without pushing or pressuring him, *the brighter and more intelligent he will become, the higher IQ he will have as an adult.*

MAYA PINES (1966): *The hottest area for research right now is not the earliest years, but the earliest months of life. Psychologists*

---

1. See Bibliography under author and date for sources of contemporary quotations. Classical allusions may be found in Bartlett's *Familiar Quotations,* unless otherwise indicated.

increasingly believe that the roots of intellectual curiosity are laid during these months. In a rich environment the child begins to get "kicks" out of learning soon after birth. If . . . all his attempts at learning are squelched, he will stop seeking this pleasure—to everyone's loss.

SIEGFRIED AND THERESE ENGELMANN (husband, Institute for Research on Exceptional Children, University of Illinois; wife, degrees in psychology and law, 1966): "The parent is not qualified to educate." *This argument is rapidly becoming obsolete as more and more educators recognize the value of preschool training. . . . the interested parent is in a far more enviable position than the schoolteacher because the parent is able to work with fewer children at a time.*

MARIA MONTESSORI (1914): *. . . The child has a personality which he is seeking to expand; he has initiative, he chooses his own work, persists in it, changes it according to his inner needs; he does not shirk effort, he rather goes in search of it, and with great joy overcomes obstacles within his capacity. He is sociable . . . wanting to share with every one his successes, his discoveries, and his little triumphs. There is therefore no need of intervention. "Wait while observing." That is the motto for the educator.*

EVELYN SHARP (teacher and writer, in a book of preschool games, 1969): *Learning specialists no longer think that in the area of mental growth we can only sit and wait, the way we wait for a child's permanent teeth to replace his baby ones. If a child is not ready for learning, we can help him to become ready. . . . By the time a child enters school, the groundwork of his education has already been laid, for better or worse. You have more influence on the development of your child's mind than any teacher ever will.*

BENJAMIN FINE (Headmaster, Sands Point [New York] Academy Country Day School for Gifted Children, journalist and educator,

1965): *In my opinion bright children are ready to enter school at about 3½ years of age.*

LOUISE BATES AMES (of the Gesell Institute of Child Development, 1967): *We think [early entrance into kindergarten programs] do harm in that they arrange for the child young in years but bright in mind . . . to be placed in a grade for which his age (and therefore in all probability his behavior level) makes him unready, even though there may be no question of his brightness.*

RUTH MARTINSON (professor whose interest in gifted education has been instrumental in forming State and national policy, in a research summary for the Report to Congress, *Education of the Gifted and Talented,* Vol. 2, 1971): *Children who read before the age of school entry, and understand mathematical concepts commonly taught to far older children, . . . also tend to be generally more mature than others of their age. It should not be necessary to retard their development until they attain an arbitrary chronological age required for school entry.*

FITZHUGH DODSON (1970): *Research . . . confirms the fact that stimulation or lack of stimulation in the early years has an important effect on adult behavior and intelligence. Dr. Benjamin Bloom, professor of psychology at the University of Chicago, has summarized a mass of research which shows that children develop 50 percent of their intelligence by the age of four.*

ARTHUR JENSEN (Professor of psychology, Berkeley, 1969): *[The] fact that half the variance in adult intelligence can be accounted for by age 4 has led to the amazing and widespread, but unwarranted and fallacious, conclusion that persons develop 50 percent of their mature intelligence by age 4!*

FITZHUGH DODSON (1970): *. . . disadvantaged children of poor parents actually enter kindergarten or first grade considerably be-*

hind in intellectual ability as compared with the children of middle class parents. And the poor children never catch up, due to the lasting effects of the lack of intellectual stimulation in their early years. This is why the Head Start programs attempt to give these children enough intellectual stimulation in their early years so that they will not be hopelessly educationally handicapped throughout their school years.

CHARLES SILBERMAN (in his 3½-year study of American schools commissioned by the Carnegie Corporation, 1970): *. . . the results of Head Start and other preschool programs [are] disappointing—initial gains seem to wash out by the second or third grade.*

EDUCATIONAL POLICIES COMMISSION, NATIONAL EDUCATION ASSOCIATION (May 1966): *All children should have the opportunity to go to school at public expense beginning at the age of four.*

Here the poor parents find themselves beleaguered by two opposing armies of experts. I used to think doctors were infallible until one told me my first son *must* be circumcised, and another said, "Do you want to mutilate him?"

I had to choose.

Pros and cons on early childhood education both make sense, however, so perhaps this choice is not a matter of life or death, either.

The kind and amount of preschool education is one of the earliest decisions parents have to make in raising a child. Oddly enough, considering parental inexperience at this point, studies have shown that gifted children are more often first or only children—although of course some geniuses do come along a lot later. Ben Franklin was the fifteenth!

Mothers are able to devote their undivided attention to a first baby, of course; this would substantiate the findings of a growing number of researchers who are concluding that human beings never learn as rapidly as they do before the age of three, and that if we start educating them in infancy we can actually affect their future IQ scores.

Ever since Alfred Binet devised a way to measure intelligence, at the beginning of this century, most children's scores have remained fairly constant, varying by no more than ten to fifteen points throughout the school career. A child was considered average, below average or retarded; or above average, superior, or highly gifted. Now they tell us parents may be able to convert children who would otherwise grow up to be of average intelligence into gifted children simply by talking to them and providing them with many different experiences while they are still in their bassinets.

Children's Centers like those at Syracuse University, New York, Chapel Hill, North Carolina, Little Rock, Arkansas, and elsewhere are teaching and testing "tiny tots" during these crucial years in the development of intelligence. And no less an authority than the Harvard Graduate School of Education admits that the mother is the "single most important environmental factor." (Isn't that a switch?) Chapter 3 will show that it has been stated frequently that 80 percent of a child's intelligence is determined *before* birth, but some dramatic changes in small children's IQs (including gains of as much as 30 points) have been effected by more intensive education—by mothers or in the Centers—than the average baby gets. Few people ever thought six- to fifteen-month-old babies *could* learn much.

On the other hand, these studies are so new that important follow-up tests are still lacking. It isn't after all so surprising that a child who has been "tutored" (as in the National Institute of Mental Health's "intelligence boosting" project under Dr. Earl Schaefer) averaged 17 points higher on IQ tests than a random sampling of three-year-olds in the same neighborhood who hadn't been taught for an hour every day for 21 months. How will these same children compare in five or ten years? In college? No doubt such follow-ups will be made, and it seems quite possible that there will be some permanent gains. I doubt if all the mothers who knock themselves out trying will turn out many more geniuses than we usually have, but it would be great if they could.

We can use all the gifted kids we can get in our increasingly complex society. Outstanding characteristics of exceptionally intelligent children are that they can work with abstract ideas, see relationships and understand new concepts; obviously these gifts will be needed more than they ever have been in the much simpler past: knowledge doubled in the decade 1950–1960; I haven't heard any estimates of what has happened to it since.

As will become apparent throughout this book, I believe a compromise can usually be effected between two extreme views, and that such a middle course will generally be the wisest. We need the Maria Montessoris to say "let them be" and the revolutionary Maya Pineses to say that millions of them will be irreparably damaged if we do let them be, in order to test out those theories and find the happy medium—the golden mean.

The inspiration for an article for *Parents Magazine,* which expresses my own feelings about early childhood education, was our youngest son, Johnny; he was gifted but, like most parents, we had not yet learned of this when he was four. I thought then, and still do, that all children are more original and imaginative before they go to school and start reading books and writing clichés.

The article is reprinted here, in part.

The Wonderful Age of Four

A four-year-old is somebody special. Not quite a baby and not quite a real little boy or girl, not quite a cherub and not quite an imp, his innocence is wondrous and his wisdom appalling!

At four he can take time out to rest from the stupendous tasks every helpless infant has to face: he has learned to walk and to talk and to act rather like other people.

In another year or so he will have to start his education and learn how to read and write and sit still in school. But nobody expects anything of him now; he doesn't even have to grow much this year—he has time. But he does have to find out about things.

That's why he asks so many questions. When he was two or three, he was just as curious, but what he wanted to know was how things feel and smell and taste; that's why he got into everything.

At four, he doesn't always need to touch all that he wonders about and his researches soar into the realm of philosophy. From somewhere, he has picked up a vocabulary that constantly amazes his parents. Use a word once in his hearing and it's his. Some evening when you tell him it's time to go to bed he will confound you by announcing, in grown-up language, "I prefer to stay up." And from this day forward your confidence in your omnipotence as a mother will be shaken: sometimes you will even doubt the truth of that comforting adage: "Mother knows best." Maybe you don't!

He will certainly inquire about the universe and who made it, where he comes from and where he is going—the idea of God is easy for him to grasp and heaven becomes, with no difficulty, the synonym for whatever makes him most happy. He does not have to see to believe. . . .

His thinking is original, not cluttered with clichés the rest of us have acquired. If you listen you will find out that often he talks in poetry.

"What do you do when you go to sleep?" someone asks him. "I dream."

"And what do you do when you wake up?"

"Turn the sunshine on!"

Stars fascinate him and he loves to wish on them. What joy when, after making a wish, he shouts, "Daddy, Daddy, that star I wished on twinkled!"

He observes, "Thunder makes a lot of noise. Lightning is not loud, but it makes the windows pretty." . . .

His logic will confound the most brilliant of scholars and woe be unto the relative who tries to tease a four-year-old. The psychologist, giving him an intelligence test, frequently gets an answer he didn't expect, though indubitably correct. "Repeat, 'I have a little dog,' " says the tester and back comes the unanswerable "I haven't. . . ."

Sometimes you may suspect he has no sense of humor; but don't you believe it. When his grandmother asks him how old he is, he says, "I am four, and how old are you?" . . . He will spend hours playing that his rocking horse is a car and the vacuum cleaner a filling station ("SSSSSS! Fill'er up!") but if you join in his pretending and suggest that a picture of a car in a magazine is real enough to ride in, he will inform you with the utmost condescension, "You can't get in it. It's just a picture." What does he believe and what doesn't he? You never know. . . .

Read him a story. He likes, he will tell you, stories about "boys and girls a-playing and a-living and a-swinging and a-do-ing." But put his name in, make him the hero of them all, because at four he sees everything with himself in the middle.

"What is a book?" you ask him.

"They're to read me a story."

"And what is a blanket?"

"A blanket is to get me snug and warm."

"What is a street?"

"A street is to keep out of so I won't get my bones all broken up."

"What is a fence?"

"To make babies stay in. . . ."

Ask any four-year-old such questions and you will get a pretty good idea of his parents, his environment, his character and anything else you want to know.

Last year you were so busy washing his pants and keeping him out of mischief that you didn't have much time left over just to talk with him and to play with him. Next year he will go to school and someone else will tell him the answers, or he will read them in a book.

But this year is yours; and your cherub, your imp, your little boy or girl belongs all day long and every day to you. It is a time of innocence, of wisdom and of wonder.

Parents' Magazine
December 1958

As may be apparent from this article I didn't believe that four-year-olds should be packed off to the rat race of school; four seemed a good year to rest after the tremendous accomplishments of learning to walk and talk which—interestingly—*all* children seem to do almost equally well in about the same period of time and without teachers. Also, for many years parents (on the whole) have done a good job during the important "first six years" which psychologists agree is "when a child's character is largely formed."

American parents would be very much against the state taking over this function (character formation), but the American public schools, with all their faults as well as virtues, are *not* political tools.

And there is the question, "What about children whose parents are not so good, or have to work?"

With more and more mothers working, especially in poorer homes where it takes two salaries to contend with the inflation, or where there is no father, day-care centers are essential, and Women's Liberationists are demanding them for wealthier career-mothers as well.

A rash of private pre-schools is breaking out all over the country even as parochial and other private schools for older children are forced to close for lack of funds. Besides day-care centers, which range from educational to custodial, nursery schools have been standard fare for many years; our children all went for one year to the college Home Economics nursery school when they were three. Its chief value was social.

Where there are good parents, with mothers at home and play-mates available but no nursery school nearby or no money for it, it's certainly a good idea to form groups of mothers who can share-the-care *and* do a little educating too. In view of the latest research findings on the pre-school intellect, we'd better! A rested mother can read to a group of children, teach them to paint or dance or speak a language, whatever each mother has to contribute —and it's all free. If you want to do this on a more ambitious scale, *Day Care: How to Plan, Develop and Operate a Day Care Center*[2] is helpful.

Early childhood education in the public schools is being tried in San Diego, in 16 multi-age classrooms for children 4 to 6; and the new "open" schools in Chula Vista, California, which are models of educational architecture, are providing for future space for pre-kindergartens, as are other school systems in the nation. Already authorities recognize the need for preschool classes for the

2. See Bibliography under Evans, Shub and Weinstein.

physically handicapped or mentally retarded, who need a longer time to prepare for first grade; this is also true for children with diverse cultural backgrounds, some of whom never even hear English spoken in their homes.

Advanced school districts provide special schools or classes or tutors for different types of handicaps; these classes are usually state-financed. Head Start is the well-known federally funded kindergarten-prep for the "disadvantaged." An admirable feature of Head Start is the involvement of parents as well as children; mothers are expected to help with the program. The chief criticism has been that the gains children make initially may be wiped out several years later, in elementary school. The Follow Up program is designed to correct this, but I wonder how often the difficulty is that the Head Start program is better, or at least more suited to these particular children, than the poorer examples of the traditional grade-school they go on to. In researching my *Creative Teaching* (1971), a book about innovations in elementary schools, I came to the conclusion after visiting the schools that were trying them out that the best things in education today are the *new* things—not without exception of course, but to a great extent.

Is this true of early childhood education? For everyone? Or for the gifted? I'm still not sure. If we are simply going to add a "grade" or two before kindergarten which is similar to the grades we already have. NO. Kids have to waste enough of the sunshine hours of their childhood as it is. If we're going to coop them up in a room all day, or even half a day, and *direct* their learning instead of leaving them free to find things out for themselves—NO. However, if small children were free to learn, each at his own pace, and to teach each other, in individualized, ungraded classes where a rich choice of activities is provided along with plenty of teachers and teacher-aides to help and guide them, starting earlier would be beneficial to many children—especially to gifted and talented boys and girls who have no such opportunities at home.

We could certainly let them start sooner on an optional basis; California State Superintendent Wilson C. Riles believes every four-year-old should have this opportunity by 1976, and the San

Diego experiment has proved popular. After two years only one of 570 children had been withdrawn in favor of the traditional classroom; of course it's a voluntary program in the first place.

Children under five are unquestionably able to learn much more than they do. Gifted children (some authorities believe average children too) can read and are probably *more ready* at two or three than when they are held back until age six. One little girl read the labels on her baby-food cans at two, and then lost interest when her parents, fearing she shouldn't learn to read so soon, let the opportunity pass. She has never been much interested in reading since, although she is now in the seventh grade—an "underachiever" with a high IQ. Compare the small boy who is happily reading at third-grade level in "independent study" in one of the experimental four- to six-year-old classrooms. He is four.

Besides the geniuses of the past who could read Greek or play concertos at age three, there are many children in our own times who have learned to type and read at that age, some by using modern technological aids like the Talking Typewriter. You can teach your own child to read, or let him teach himself, and it is no longer considered so reprehensible as it was before Sputnik. Oddly enough, early reading is a distinguishing trait of gifted children mentioned more often than early speaking, although of course larger vocabularies are typical of the gifted when they do speak. It is not uncommon for a very bright child to say nothing at all until age four, and then open his mouth and spout paragraphs!

But, if your child does show early signs of being gifted and you want to help him, or her, develop those gifts, you'll have to resign yourself to a great deal of criticism even though, in this generation, you can also find some support. Audrey Grost's *Genius in Residence,* which tells about her son Mike's early childhood years and what the neighbors said, is one of the most entertaining books a mother with same problems could read. It's *never* easy. The story of Friedrich Froebel, who founded the first kindergartens in Germany in 1836, sounds like that of a revolutionary educator today. He too believed that education should begin at birth, that teachers and parents should allow children to follow the lines of their own interest, that *planned* play and games can teach as well as amuse. And he too was fiercely opposed; in 1851 a law was passed forbidding the establishment of kindergartens!

Maria Montessori is more popular today than ever, although she developed her ideas about the education of preschool children in 1906, in Italy, and they soon became popular in other countries, too. She believed it important to develop the child's senses in the years from 1½ to 5, and, as in the English nursery and infant schools, she used plenty of concrete materials, including her famous "Children's House." The important consideration was *self-education;* the children were in charge of the house, objects in it were breakable, and the children were not told "Don't touch!"

They learned because things broke.

The giant figure in educational psychology today is Jean Piaget; he has probably had more influence on educators than any thinker since John Dewey. And he formed his ideas on early childhood education, as all parents should, on *his own children,* and others with whom he shot marbles while asking questions.

Mothers and fathers who spend time with their children every day, talking to them, reading with them, playing games, listening to music or a good TV show, taking walks or visiting museums, can teach their small ones more than they would learn in a school. Many years ago my husband took our oldest daughter, then four, to an opera.

"What was that opera you took Frea to?" I asked him just now.

When he didn't remember, I called her up (she has children of her own now). "Oh, it was Carmen," she said. "That was so much fun."

I remember Johnny in his bassinet at five weeks refusing to go to sleep to anything but *classical* records; Daddy reading a rumbly Pooh and a squeaky Piglet, and playing the piano for us all to sing out of *The Fireside Book of Folk-Songs.*

History and geography on trips in our old Packard: once we were driving through the Southern states and talking about the Civil War. Our second daughter, Sheila Mary—then about nine— read a sign on a store.

"Who was General Merchandise?" she asked.

Serious discussions with our philosophical four-year-olds:

"How was I started?"

"What does God stand on?"

"If everybody in the world was good, we wouldn't need any policemen, would we?"

For the children of parents who can't—or won't—provide that kind of early childhood education, we do need schools. But not just an extension of the long, dull years from "K through 12." Children, all children but especially the gifted, should be allowed to learn as much as they want to, as fast as they want to—

And as soon as they want to.

That's the only way they ever *will* want to.

2

Is Special Education for the Gifted Undemocratic?

MRS. NORMAL: *Why should my taxes be spent for special education for your child?*

MRS. BRIGHT: *Many authorities agree that gifted students can do the work in from one to three years less time. One year's schooling in the U.S. costs about $15 billion. So if my child can get through school faster, that will save taxes.*

MRS. NORMAL: *She can't get through faster. That's undemocratic!*

PLATO (a deep voice from the 4th century B.C., chuckling): *Democracy . . . is a charming form of government, full of variety and disorder, and dispensing a sort of equality to equals and unequals alike.*

THOMAS JEFFERSON: *We must dream of an aristocracy of achievement arising out of a democracy of opportunity.*

JAMES RUSSELL LOWELL: *It was in making education not only common to all, but in some sense compulsory on all, that the destiny of the free republics of America was practically settled.*

SAMUEL BUTLER (19th-century English writer, painter and composer): *I do not think America is a good place in which to be a genius.*

BERTRAND RUSSELL (English philosopher, 1926): *The American public schools achieve successfully a task never before attempted on a large scale; the task of transforming a heterogeneous selection of mankind into a homogeneous nation.*

JOHN CURTIS GOWAN (professor, writer and president of the National Association for Gifted Children, with George Demos, 1964): *How do we harmonize the opposing principles of developing each individual to his maximum and at the same time provide for the greatest general good through a common education?*

ALFRED GITELSON (Judge, County of Los Angeles Superior Court, Case 822854): *Equal education is the foundation of the right to be a human being. . . . This does not mean that any gifted child or any child having a greater ability to learn may or shall be deprived of his or her opportunity to learn to the best of his or her ability. That opportunity must be made available to all on equal terms.*

JEROME BRUNER (educator and writer, 1960): *One thing seems clear: if all students are helped to the full utilization of their intellectual powers, we will have a better chance of surviving as a democracy in an age of enormous technological and social complexity.*

RUTH STRANG (Professor of Education, 1960): *Democracy requires diversity rather than uniformity. Valuable individual differences need to be cultivated. . . . Few people object to making special provisions for the athlete, or for the handicapped child. Gifted children may become handicapped if appropriate provision is not made for them.*

BERTRAND RUSSELL (1926): *It would be disastrous to insist upon a dead level of uniformity. Some boys and girls . . . can derive more benefit from higher education. . . . In higher education, exceptional opportunity for exceptional ability is indispensable.*

JOHN W. GARDNER (former President of the Carnegie Corporation and Secretary of Health, Education and Welfare, 1961): *Those who are most deeply devoted to a democratic society must be precisely the ones who insist upon excellence. . . . The idea for which this nation stands will not survive if the highest goal men set for themselves is an amiable mediocrity.*

JOHN HOLT (teacher and writer, 1970): *Human experience, knowledge, culture is everyone's. No one ought to have to prove that he deserves it. It ought to have been used for a great upward leveling, to make a universal aristocracy of wisdom and learning. It was and is used instead to make a hierarchy, a pyramid of men, with the learned men self-placed at the top.*

There is something to be said for both positions, but recently a new dimension has been added to the discussion which may resolve the conflict. It may *not* be democratic to devote special attention and state and federal funds to "the gifted" if we continue to find most of these children in wealthy and/or professional families. Studies consistently show that the great majority of the "identified gifted" come from "high socioeconomic communities."

We are just beginning to realize that there are *undiscovered* talents and leadership, even more in need of development, in our slums and ghettoes, in poor rural communities or in families that are always on the move.

"Give me your tired, your poor, your huddled masses yearning to breathe free" was inscribed on the Statue of Liberty in New York harbor in 1908, yet we have huddled masses yearning to breathe free in all our cities today. In our plans to educate the gifted we must include talented and creative citizens who can't pass the mental-cultural tests we have so long used as the sole criteria for success—in school and in life.

If we can find and educate *all* our potential leaders to the high limits they can reach if encouraged by recognition and given the *freedom to learn,* then we will have a genuine democracy, with equal opportunity for leaders from every community.

But from *every* community—we must be careful not to go to an opposite extreme and underrate the vital contributions of the too-often unjustly resented "élite." They have contributed and will continue to contribute much to human knowledge, comfort and enjoyment of life for everyone: a telescope (Galileo's father was a wealthy merchant), a treatment or cure for a formerly fatal disease, a symphony—or a television set. TV *is* a "cultural background." We can't ignore it. We should *use* it, and try to improve it.

Geniuses are a minority, no matter what color they are; the number of geniuses is estimated at one-half to one percent of the total population, although the gifted and talented may include from 20 to 30 percent, depending on what criteria are used; new kinds of tests, such as nonverbal tests for creativity, will increase the percentage, and perhaps some genius will devise a way in which we could all become geniuses.

Experiments in this field are already under way (asexual reproduction, DNA, RNA—and how about brain transplants?) I can't say I'm in any hurry for this millennium; one of the most fascinating things in creation is our individual differences. But we're going to need all the gifts we've got, and with the spiralling complexity of our society we can use more geniuses than ever before, as well as plenty of good and intelligent people to carry out their ideas.

Opal DiMatteo, a high school counselor, says "the gifted kid is the neglected kid. Gifted kids are turning off all over." And her school is in an "advantaged" district.

We can't discriminate against a child because his family has money or high social position, no matter how strongly we feel that it's time to help those who haven't any such advantages to obtain them. We can't (as some do) use this as an *excuse* to do nothing for "the rich kids." (Who wants to pass the plate for Howard Hughes, as someone put it!) Oddly enough, it isn't so much the poor that take this attitude as it is the equally well-to-do anti-intellectual. And the "rich kids" aren't always rich in money.

In this book we'll look at programs and ideas for ALL the gifted, as many as we can find; and we'll discuss new ways of finding them. Federal funds and popular opinion currently favor the children who have been deprived so long because of poverty or prejudice, so this is an especially opportune time to help them, and to foster this spirit so it will be continued long enough to get substantial results.

Justice has a pair of scales that sometimes has to be overloaded on one side in order to compensate for the fact that it was formerly overloaded on the other. The basic democratic sense of fair play among the majority of Americans is finally coming to the surface, although we live in a period of dissatisfaction for people who feel we are doing too little—or on the other hand too much—for racial minorities. A meeting of the minds of our brightest boys and girls from all communities could eliminate the "race problem"—eventually—altogether.

Dr. David Hermanson, District Coordinator of Secondary Gifted Programs in the San Diego City Schools, is working toward this ideal through independent study centers and other interesting programs at junior and senior high schools, while Mrs. Evelyn Curry, Coordinator of the Elementary Gifted, oversees "clusters" of both IQ and "site-identified" children, and plans special activities for them. In disadvantaged areas, where there are not so many high IQs, students are site-identified for outstanding qualities of leadership and creativity. In some cases this results in children from different communities sharing the same "center" schools; where it does not, Dr. Hermanson has a good idea.

"We need field trips for the independent study groups," he says. "I don't mean just going to the zoo! Let's send bus loads of the gifted kids—the leaders—from one school to have seminars, share ideas, with the gifted kids in other schools." This would be a type of busing it would be hard to find fault with. Dr. Hermanson is also working on opportunities for the gifted to travel in other parts of America, and abroad.

Professor E. Paul Torrance of the University of Georgia, whose name has become a byword for *creativity,* says that in the future we'll have to depend on gifted members of disadvantaged and minority cultures for most of our creative achievements.

Larry McElroy, a concerned teacher of educationally handicapped children, explains this: "Why do we expect to find the leaders and creative artists of the future among the minority cultures? Because they're hungry. They're hungry for the self-image, the material security, the upward mobility.

"What does a rich kid want? They grow up with everything. There's no tension, no problems to solve. They seem like they're in a vacuum—they float.

"But the deprived—not all of them, the creative ones—have a deep rage, and a need to express this rage."

Can they do it? Yes, with help, although the creative arts may not be the best path to *material* security. Creative minds are needed in all fields, however, not only in poetry and painting. But the "rich kids" are needed too. Professor Lewis Terman's Stanford follow-up studies of 1000 gifted California children of the 1920s to mid-life in the 1950s show that 45 percent of the men are now in the professions and 26 percent in important semi-professional and business positions. Of the 48 percent full-time employed women, 61 percent were in professions, 35 percent in business. What would we do without such leaders?

Even more important, perhaps, in this age of "enormous technological and social complexity," will be the one in a hundred thousand to one in a million mentally gifted kids—the geniuses. As James B. Conant and others have pointed out, the highly gifted are an entirely different group from the academically talented and should be treated quite differently; but this distinction is seldom made—"the gifted" with IQs of from 120 or so to 200 are usually grouped together in spite of their different needs and potential contributions. We need the most complex brains as well as the highly creative to sort out the tangle of new knowledge and invention.

Now, when changes are exploding all around us whether we

like them or not; when our latest younger generation has expressed frustration and disillusionment to the point of destruction and despair; now we need a new generation of creative thinkers and dreamers from all our communities to plan and *construct* an orderly world of tomorrow.

This new generation has to come from the gifted children of today.

3
Who *Are* the Gifted?

ALFRED BINET (co-originator, in 1905, of the individual intelligence tests still most widely used to determine IQ—intelligence quotient): *. . . a father and mother who raise a child themselves, who watch over him and study him fondly, would have great satisfaction in knowing that the intelligence of a child can be measured, and would willingly make the effort to find out if their own child is intelligent.*

ARTHUR JENSEN (1969): *[The Binet-Simon intelligence test] is now regarded as one of the major "breakthroughs" in the history of psychology.*

JOHN CURTIS GOWAN AND GEORGE DEMOS (1964): *A value judgment must be made by the school district on . . . what it means by a "gifted child." . . . Taking a norm population and using the Stanford-Binet, the mean I.Q. equals 100. . . . The cut score of intelligence tests for identifying gifted children has often been set at 140 I.Q. after Terman (1925). . . . I.Q. 130 . . . has been accepted as a base by numerous schools. . . . Some school systems cut at 120 I.Q. which identifies 10.5 percent and the recommendation of the NEA Conference on Academically Gifted and Talented recommended a cut at . . . 116 I.Q. The trend has been toward a broader definition of giftedness with lower acceptable levels for the cut-off point.* [See Gowan below.]

WILLARD ABRAHAM (educator and writer, 1958): *We cannot and should not tell a parent an exact IQ. The reason is simple—there is no such thing.*

THE EDITORS OF THE *Atlantic* (September 1971): *IQ tests and their like have become controversial, in spite of the hundreds of millions of them still given around the world. . . . lately in America . . . public discussion of intelligence requires physical not to mention intellectual, courage, for the subject is close to taboo.*

DANIEL J. BOORSTIN (historian and satirist, 1971): *. . . as many social scientists have come to believe, the IQ is* merely *quantitative and self-confirming ("Intelligence tests test what intelligence tests test.")* [Edwin G. Boring]

ARTHUR JENSEN (1969): *Had the first IQ tests been devised in a hunting culture, "general intelligence" might well have turned out to involve visual acuity and running speed rather than vocabulary and symbol manipulation.*

JOHN CURTIS GOWAN (in a speech in San Diego January 31, 1972): *IQ giftedness is an outmoded concept.*

JOAN BECK (*Chicago Tribune* staff journalist, columnist, and mother, 1967): *In one research project, in which the I.Q.'s of 152 children were tested repeatedly between the ages of twenty-one months and eighteen years, two youngsters showed increases of 70 and 79 points.* [See Honzik, in Bibliography.] *This is enough difference to move a youngster from the general classification of "educable mentally retarded" to "gifted." The scores of two other youngsters in this long-term study group decreased about the same amount. . . . One changed as much as 50 points and several as much as 30 points between the ages of six and eight. . . . Similar changes in children's I.Q.'s have been noted in many other research studies, particularly when youngsters under age six are involved.*

RUTH MARTINSON (from her research summary compiled for the U.S. Office of Education, in the Report to Congress, *Education of the Gifted and Talented,* Vol. 2, 1971): *Identification of the gifted and talented in different parts of the country has been piecemeal, sporadic, and sometimes nonexistent. . . . Special injustice has occurred through apathy toward certain minorities, although neglect of the gifted in this country is a universal and increasing problem.*

J. P. GUILFORD (psychologist noted for his work on the structure of the intellect, in *The Gifted Child Quarterly,* Vol. 6, 1962): *. . . selection on the basis of IQ alone will definitely miss many potentially gifted children. . . . Although about 60 primary intellectual abilities have now been demonstrated, the number of these for which there are available tests is much smaller.*

E. PAUL TORRANCE (in *The Gifted Child Quarterly,* Vol. 12, 1968): *. . . if one uses only an intelligence test and therefore identifies the upper twenty percent as gifted, he would miss seventy percent of those who would be identified as falling in the top twenty percent on tests of creative thinking ability.*

FRANK RIESSMAN (professor and author of noted books in sociology, 1968): *We've neglected the huge pool of gifted individuals among the poor. This is not a few people—thousands of people in the disadvantaged and ghetto areas are being screened out.*

WILLARD ABRAHAM (1968): *The emphases on individualized instruction, behavioral objectives and programmed learning and computer-managed instruction . . . all that brings us far from the gobbledygook of superficial enrichment, identification and definition of who is talented or gifted of a few years ago.*[1]

---

1. The statements of Mr. Riessman and Mr. Abraham were contributed to Charles Bish's "What's New in Education for the Gifted," *Accent on Talent,* vol. 2, 1968.

MARLAND, SIDNEY P., JR. (Definition of "gifted and talented" established by the advisory panel for the Commissioner of Education pursuant to Public Law 91-230, Section 806, for purposes of Federal education programs in the 1971 Report to Congress): *Gifted and talented children are those identified by professionally qualified persons who by virtue of outstanding abilities, are capable of high performance. These are children who require differentiated educational programs and/or services beyond those normally provided by the regular school program in order to realize their contribution to self and society.*

Children capable of high performance include those with demonstrated achievement and/or potential ability in any of the following areas, singly or in combination:

1. *general intellectual ability*
2. *specific academic aptitude*
3. *creative or productive thinking*
4. *leadership ability*
5. *visual and performing arts*
6. *psychomotor ability*

CECIL MUNSEY (Writer, District Resource Teacher and editor of San Diego City Schools' *Programs for the Gifted Bulletin*, Spring 1971): *A recent national survey by the U.S. Office of Education has revealed that 57 percent of the nation's schools claim they don't have any gifted children.*

Ricky Ponce de Leon is a musical genius. According to Robert D. Shushan, an executive director of the Exceptional Children's Foundation, he has an IQ of 55. Yet he plays the organ and the piano, guitar and several other instruments, has composed many songs, and knows about 1000 songs by heart. At nineteen he gave organ concerts in Los Angeles, San Francisco and Sacramento, and plays in a night club in Manila, where he lives.

Anne Sullivan, who was later to become Helen Keller's

"Teacher," was beaten by her parents and sent to a poorhouse after their death; almost blind herself, she couldn't read or write until she was sent to Perkins Institute for the Blind; by fifteen she was teaching Greek history to a class of ten-year-olds. Her gift for teaching is legendary now.

Who are the gifted? It's sometimes hard to tell.

A mother I know was puzzled by her only child, born when she was almost forty. She soon suspected, but it took her over three years to establish the fact that he was not, as some people thought, mentally retarded but actually a gifted child. Later tests revealed that he was highly gifted, with an IQ above 170.

John Curtis Gowan and George Demos, in the most thorough discussion of *The Education and Guidance of the Ablest* (511 pages) that I came across in my research include the following figures on above-average ability in terms of the *Stanford-Binet* IQ. Other tests yield so-called IQs which vary from these norms, but the Stanford-Binet has been the most widely-accepted scale for over fifty years:

a) *The academically talented:* above 115 IQ (16 percent of population).
b) *The superior:* above 125 IQ (5 percent of population).
c) *The gifted* (Terman's use): above 140 IQ (0.6 percent of population).
d) *The highly gifted:* above 160 IQ (0.007 percent of population).

Thus, the highly gifted would be one of 70 or fewer persons per million; an amusing example these authors cite is an 18-month-old baby who could beat his parents at double solitaire. (You might try this game if you just can't wait to find out if your child is a genius!)

Thomas and Crescimbeni's helpful paperback, *Guiding the Gifted Child,* tabulates the following statistics based on a population of 200 million:

below 60 IQ, *trainable:* .6 percent (1.2 million people).
60–69 IQ, *educable:* 2.0 percent (4 million people).
70–79 IQ, *very slow learners and high educables:* 5.6 percent (11.2 million people).

80–89 IQ, *low average or slow learners:* 14.5 percent (29 million people).

90–99 IQ, *average learners:* 23 percent (46 million people).

100–109 IQ, *average learners:* 23.5 percent (47 million people).

110–119 IQ, *high average, bright and fast learners:* 18.1 percent (36.2 million people).

120–129 IQ, *superior:* 8.2 percent (16.4 million people)

130–139 IQ, *gifted to highly gifted:* 3.1 percent (6.2 million people).

140 IQ or above, *highly gifted to genius:* 1.0–1.5 percent (2 million to 3 million people).

These authors conclude that one in a million individuals may have an IQ of 180. Parents of these most highly gifted children (180–200) are sometimes told, "The scale didn't go high enough to measure your child."

Should parents be told their child's IQ? Traditionally, the great majority of educators say *no,* but, as may be noted in the controversy at the beginning of this chapter, there is a highly regarded and intelligent minority who say parents *should* be told. Probably, if you are reading this book, and your child is gifted, you'll know it! As to the "exact" IQ, that may well vary; and the parent who has been given a figure may be tempted to compare notes with other parents, sometimes with painful social results for the child. So if you do know the "awe-ful truth," as I for one believe you have a "right" to, better keep it to yourself.

Teachers are usually given access to this information when it's available; of course the expense of individual testing means that many children, particularly those who don't seem especially bright or especially slow, never get tested for IQ, unless their parents arrange to have it done themselves. Occasionally this is a good idea, if only for the parents' own peace of mind.

When one child in the family is gifted, and studies have shown this is frequently the oldest, parents sometimes expect too much of their other children; to be sure, it's common for more than one child in a family to be gifted, and in some cases a parent may *overlook* a younger gifted or talented child. Psychologists emphatically agree that intelligence *can* be measured, so IQ tests can help parents avoid expecting too much *or* too little of each individual child in the family.

It is often said that teachers overlook gifted children because they are shy on the one hand, or badly behaved on the other; however, authorities agree that highly intelligent students as a rule compare favorably with the general population socially and emotionally as well as physically. *Ordinarily* the gifted child stands out in the crowd; you can't miss him—or her—whether or not you know his IQ. Some people, unfortunately, feel that such children *should* be ignored—"for their own sakes."

The 1971 Report to Congress, quoted above, states in no uncertain terms that they should *not* be ignored—for all our sakes.

The first step toward developing the talents of our children is to find them—as early as possible. Ever since Alfred Binet, at the turn of this century, found a way to test mental ability, we have been using his tests, as revised by Lewis Terman of Stanford University, and similar tests, to give a numerical score to the intelligence of school children.

Binet's original motive for working the tests out, with his colleague, Théodore Simon, in France, had nothing to do with "gifted" students. He was concerned with vindicating falsely labeled "retarded" children who—solely on the basis of opinion and guesswork—were denied an education. Imagine the indignation of an American parent if he were told his child was not smart enough to go to school, and his relief when tests were devised by which mental ability could be *proved*. Also, in cases where children actually are retarded, it's a good thing to know to what extent, what can be expected of them, and what kind of education they should have.

Although special education for the retarded at two levels (the trainable below 50 and the educable at about 75 and below) outnumber special gifted programs in the United States, from about 1916 on a natural interest in the children who scored high on these tests led to the establishment of a numerical definition of mental giftedness. Professor Terman's study of 1000 California children of 140 and above IQ is probably the most fascinating and complete follow-up of any group of human beings over such a long period of time (*Genetic Studies of Genius,* Stanford, California, Stanford University Press, 1925, 1926, 1930, 1947, 1959—see Bibliography for volume titles).

But any cutoff score on intelligence tests will exclude many children with high potential as creative thinkers, leaders, athletic champions (the Greeks never called *their* athletes dumb!), mechanical geniuses, mentally or physically handicapped musicians or artists, and an assortment of other potentially outstanding citizens who can't do all the tasks on the tests.

These tasks include memory (repeat five numbers, forward and backward, or sentences); logic (fold and cut a paper and tell how many holes will be in it without unfolding it); vocabulary; reading, and reading comprehension; rhyming words; drawing or fitting geometrical forms, to mention a few. Since school districts and states which have special programs for the gifted often require the child to have a certain score, which varies as we have seen from 116 to 140 or higher in different localities, boys and girls with outstanding talents are often left out.

This is compounded by the fact that unrecognized but common physical disabilities, such as partial deafness, *petit mal,* or eye disorders, would affect scores on any test. Emotional upsets on the day of testing, on the part of either testee or tester, lack of discipline or concentration, inefficient testers—there are so many things that can deny a child who *is* gifted his right to profit by education especially designed for him. He needs it even more than does the child who is good at passing intelligence tests and influencing teachers by a pleasant personality and no problems.

Not—let there be no question about this—that it is possible to do well on these tests *without* exceptional mental ability. Studies have been made which concur in the finding that while study or coaching may raise a score 10 or 15 points at most, this is about the same "spread" that we get in testing the same child on different days; this varies for physical, emotional and other reasons, such as rapport with the tester.

An understandable human reaction occurs when a bright boy

or girl who does consistently good work in school is denied the privilege of being in a gifted group. One frustrated mother had a daughter who kept testing at 128, even when tests were repeated; the cutoff score was 132.

"Some day you'll know how it feels to have a gifted child that nobody can identify!" This mother told the young lady psychologist who tested her daughter the third time.

That's a funny story, but if you think about it, you don't laugh. An IQ of 128 indicates superior mental ability, and combined with industry and desire, that girl could handle the work in a gifted program better than a pupil with an IQ of 160 if he were *not* industrious or interested. If I could have my pick of children to bring up or teach, generally speaking I'd choose the ones with IQs between about 120 and 140. Other teachers agree they are usually a joy. But let's not "put down" our geniuses, either.

Just as we should aim at including the more-difficult-to-identify "disadvantaged" children who have gifts to offer our democracy, so should we try to include *all* the bright children who would benefit by the freedom and stimulation of special education for the "deprived" gifted, not just some of them.

What about those "creative" kids we've been excluding? As Professor Torrance says, hundreds of studies, like those of Jacob Getzels and Philip Jackson in 1962, have shown that 70 percent of the children who score in the top 20 percent on tests of creative thinking ability will not be identified as gifted (in the top 20 percent) on the basis of intelligence tests. Creativity, then, is not the same *kind* of intellectual ability as that measured by the traditional mental tests; but certainly it is a function, and one of a very high order indeed, of the mind.

During the past decade, interest in creativity has flourished. J. P. Guilford's famous cubic model of "the structure of the intellect" (1961) led to the fascinating "Williams Cube" (see Frank E. Williams, "Models for Encouraging Creativity in the Classroom," *Educational Technology Magazine,* December 1969, reprinted in Gowan and Torrance's *Educating the Ablest,* 1971).

E. Paul Torrance of Georgia, Al Hatch of the Los Angeles City

Schools, and George Witt, working with disadvantaged students in New Haven, Connecticut, have devised pictorial and figural, nonverbal or at least partially nonverbal tests and games for identifying the creatively gifted. Best known of these new tests are the Torrance Tests of Creative Thinking, published by Personnel Press, Princeton, New Jersey. Dawn Shulman, a San Diego elementary school teacher who has been trying Al Hatch's picture-tests in disadvantaged areas, says this kind of test is great fun to give— and to take. Also, it has psychological values for the child over and above the identification procedure.

Questions like "What is creativity?" and "How can it be developed?" would require not only a separate chapter but another book to answer. Examples of creatively gifted children and samples of their work (art, writing, ideas) would fill an encyclopedia. Regretfully, I must limit myself to a final recommendation for the identification of creative children so that they may benefit from any special programs their school system offers for the gifted.

Since, as at least some authorities agree, a good deal of the mental ability which "intelligence tests test" is required for most creative thinking and any *useful* creative production; since, that is, creative ability and intelligence do at least overlap—why not lower the required cutoff score on IQ tests for children who demonstrate unusual creativity? (Then maybe that little girl with the IQ of 128 would finally make it!) The tendency to lower cutoff scores has already been remarked by Professor Gowan, and children of above-average mental ability (over 110) who exhibit high creative thinking ability or artistic expression should do well in special programs designed to help them develop their talents. Children of average or below average mental ability might well have difficulty in keeping up with the extra work such programs encourage, although there will always be exceptions.

The lower cutoff score for the creative would also allow some leeway for the culturally disadvantaged child, who may have a higher IQ than he can demonstrate on a "white middle-class standardized" intelligence test. On the other hand, children who did not demonstrate any special creative ability or productive talent would probably not be happy in gifted programs unless they demonstrated superior intellectual ability by higher scores on the Stanford-Binet.

Unfortunately the number-one complaint in most school systems is that they can't afford to educate all the gifted they've already got, let alone go around looking for any more of them!

The 1971 Report to Congress based on extensive investigation by a federal task force from the Office of Education, with the cooperation of outstanding educators in the gifted field in many states, disclosed a "nationwide neglect of the gifted." The Congress itself under the leadership of Senator Jacob Javits (R., N. Y.) and Representative John Erlenborn (R., Ill.) asked for the report in 1969, and the recommendations for doing something about this neglect include placing the responsibility under the Bureau of Education for the Handicapped, with the admonition that funds for the gifted will be kept separate from funds for other kinds of handicapped children. So "handicapped" has become the latest "in" word for bright children, taking the place of "exceptional" now that "exceptional" has come to mean physically or mentally disabled to the general public; the gifted have been and still are included under Exceptional Child Services in school districts which offer these helpful programs, but in most states the notion still persists that geniuses and other above average individuals don't need any help.

The Report to Congress revealed that almost half of the states have no state personnel in charge of gifted youth education; that only seventeen states and Puerto Rico have full-time Department of Education personnel; and that even where provisions are made, only a handful of the states have made more than a token effort. This was the survey where 57 percent of the nation's principals reported *no* gifted children in their schools! Yet the most conservative estimate is that 3 percent—3 in 100—of the total school population is gifted (for a total of 1.5 million children); many estimates are much higher.

There seem to be two major problems. First, in order to educate any of the gifted more nearly up to their potential ability to learn, we have to overcome opposition from the community—and this is true of almost every community. Too often active opposition or apathy, or a misunderstanding of the nature and needs of bright children are also found among Boards of Education, superintendents, principals and teachers also, even among *gifted* teaching and administrative personnel!

"I believe they should all stay in high school until they are eighteen," a counselor of 250 gifted students told me the other day, although most authorities agree that some acceleration is advisable for boys and girls who plan to go on to graduate studies. (It's a good idea to get an M.D. or Ph.D. *before* starting a family, but mentally superior boys and girls fall in love just as soon as everyone else.)

Other advisers of gifted students make much of their "emotional problems" even though studies for many years have shown that the gifted generally have fewer rather than more emotional problems than the average student. The highly gifted seem to have more than the moderately gifted; this is often due to boredom in schools which give them no chance to *use* their remarkable brains.

The second major problem is that in order to educate *more* gifted students we need more money: for teachers for smaller classes, psychologists for identification, books and other educational materials, field trips, further pilot programs to find out the best ways to do what has never been done before. My psychology professor used to tell us psychology was a science in rompers; programs for the gifted are still in diapers. But there are some exciting things happening here and there, and another need for money that the Report to Congress uncovered is for the dissemination of these ideas. That is my major purpose in writing this book, as well as my earlier *Creative Teaching,* about innovative programs in elementary schools. I'm a self-constituted public relations person for better education.

Recently I suggested to a member of the Board of Education that money spent on programs that would result in the acceleration of our more able pupils would be more than replaced by the money saved by their getting through school in fewer years.

"We wouldn't want to do *that* to them just to *save money*," he replied in horror.

"We'd be doing it to help them," I persisted. "The money we saved would be incidental."

In any case the two major problems form a circle which we hope won't be a vicious one. *The more money we can get, the more children we can identify as gifted,* always remembering that far less is or is likely to be spent on the gifted than on the physically or mentally handicapped. In turn, *the higher percentage of population we can help by special education for the gifted, the less opposition there will be from the community,* and the more support and approval they will give.

The ideal would be that all children who wanted the extra learning would be given the chance to participate (self-identification); those who don't want it would be more likely to call it extra *work*. More and more tests which do not emphasize the intellect are being devised, such as the Torrance Tests of Creative Thinking and Al Hatch's HISC. (See "Identifying Potential Giftedness," by Mary Meeker in the National Association of Secondary School Principals *Bulletin,* December 1971 or write Al Hatch, Los Angeles City Schools, Zone D, Los Angeles, California and ask for a copy). Such tests should not be used instead of mental tests, of course, but in addition to them.

Site identification is often used to involve more children from deprived communities: teachers who have had the opportunity to observe the children over a period of time know if they have talents or unusual ability in some field. Fred L. Strodtbeck of the University of Chicago says deprived children often have math and verbal skills, and that Negro girls especially could be trained for math careers. One of the many kinds of special education for outstanding boys and girls is on-the-job training (while still in school) for professional, scientific, technical, business and other careers which would be of benefit to both individual and society.

Perhaps we're only getting around to the inescapable conclusion that all children are gifted, and that in order to develop the particular gifts of each one, we have to make some long overdue changes in our artificial mass methods of education. These changes are already in operation; pilot schools and classes all over the country are demonstrating the value and practicability of *individualized* learning, which is the key to freedom.

We must break the molds we've been pouring children into, and let each child learn in his own way and at his own time, as he did so successfully when he learned to walk and to talk. This is the only way we'll ever be able to "identify" *all* the gifted, and help them learn all they can learn—with joy.

4

Intelligence — Born or Bred?

SIR FRANCIS GALTON (1869): *Where the allowance granted by nature is inadequate, the keenest will and the stoutest industry will strive in vain.*

LEWIS TERMAN AND MELITA ODEN (1947): *That superior achievement tends to run in families has been noted by all students of genius.*

GENE R. HAWES (in a book on testing, 1964): *To this day the question has not been answered in favor of either "nature" or "nurture" as the prime source of intelligence. The best answer seems to be "both" in unknown proportions.*

ARTHUR JENSEN (1969): . . . *we see that the correlation between identical or monozygotic (MZ) twins reared apart is .75.* [See Figure 6, page 50 and other Tables in his *Harvard Educational Review* article for illustrations of his estimates.] *Since MZ twins develop from a single fertilized ovum and thus have exactly the same genes, any difference between the twins must be due to non-genetic factors. And if they are reared apart in uncorrelated environments, the difference between a perfect correlation (1.00) and the obtained correlation (.75) gives an estimate of the proportion of the variance in IQs attributable to environmental differences: 1.00 — 0.75 = 0.25. Thus 75 percent of the variance can be said to be due to genetic variation . . . and 25 percent to environmental variation. Now let us go to the opposite extreme and look at unrelated children reared together. They have no genetic inheritance*

55

*in common, but they are reared in a common environment. There-
fore the correlation between such children will reflect the environment. . . . the proportion of IQ variance due to environment is
.24; and the remainder, 1.00 — .24 = 76 is due to heredity. There
is quite good agreement between the two estimates of heritability.*
[His final estimate including all kinship correlations is .81, the
widely quoted "80%" inherited.]

CHARLES B. SILBERMAN (1970): . . . *Jensen's argument that black-
white IQ differences are largely genetic in origin simply does not
stand. As Jencks points out* [Christopher Jencks in *The New Republic*, Sept. 13, 1969] *something like one-sixth of the white identical twins reared in separate homes have as large a difference in
IQ—15 points or thereabouts—as that between the average white
and the average black. The differences between the twins can be
due only to environment, since identical twins always have the
same genes.*

LEWIS TERMAN AND MELITA ODEN (1947): *The ancestral strains
[of 1528 children of IQ 135–200 selected for a study of gifted
traits] stem back to all the European countries, and to China,
Japan, the Philippines, Mexico, Black Africa, and Pre-Columbian
America. No race or nationality has any monopoly on brains.*

CHRISTOPHER JENCKS (psychologist and writer, 1969): *Jewish
children . . . do better on IQ tests than Christians at the same
socioeconomic level, but very few people conclude that Jews are
genetically superior to Christians.*

CHARLES SILBERMAN (1970): *Given the present state of knowledge among geneticists, biologists, psychologists and anthropolo-
gists, we simply do not know whether blacks and whites have
different gene pools with respect to IQ—nor do we know whether
such differences, if they exist, favor one group or the other. Indeed,
given the social and cultural environment with which black Americans have had to contend, it is quite possible that they are genetically superior to whites.*

LETA HOLLINGWORTH (psychometrist and writer, 1942): *Dixon and Hirsh offer the hypothesis that racial mixture is an antecedent of genius.*

GEORGE I. THOMAS AND JOSEPH CRESCIMBENI (professors and writers on education for the gifted, 1966): *Although a much higher number of gifted children can be identified on the basis of family . . . and cultural background, teachers should not make the assumption that bright children will not be found coming from poor homes or from families where one or both parents have little if any education.*

AUDREY GROST (mother of a genius—1970): *Our progressive educators are as appalled with the expected population explosion of genius intelligence in these [concentrated scientific] communities as they are with the waste in the ghetto.*

JAMES MCPARTLAND (in *The Johns Hopkins Magazine,* April 1970): *Studies have been conducted in the past few years by researchers at Johns Hopkins using the data . . . collected for the Coleman Report on equality of educational opportunity. . . . The Johns Hopkins studies showed that the difference in achievement between the average Negro in a segregated classroom and his counterpart in a mostly white classroom is on the order of one-half standard deviation . . . [i.e.] desegregation serves to cut the racial achievement gap in half. The longer the Negro student spends in a desegregated situation, the more dramatic the improvement in achievement.*

At this point you may add a few recent quotes on school busing, pro and con. This is one of the bitterest controversies of our times, but this debate does seem preferable at least to the situation in not-so-former times, when buses were segregated into front and back.

Peace.

Closely akin to the dispute over "Is special education for the gifted undemocratic?" is the dispute about heredity versus environment in the creation and/or development of a child's mind. Commonly known as the nature-nurture controversy, this dispute has been going on for many years. Its famous forerunner, Sir Francis Galton's *Hereditary Genius, An Inquiry into Its Laws and Consequences,* was published in 1869, and is available in a World Book Publishing Company edition, 1962.

In the past few years much fiery discussion has centered around the theories of William B. Shockley, Arthur Jensen and others, which not only set forth the conclusion that intelligence is largely hereditary (the figure is often stated as 80 percent) but extrapolates from this that an entire race might be inferior in intelligence to another. In certain studies, Negroes scored about fifteen points lower than Caucasians, on the average, but this can reasonably be attributed to the typically different environment. In that environment can be found factors ranging from nutrition to a different cultural background which job and other discrimination in the past century and more has forced upon black people.

The Supreme Court's 1954 decision, the Freedom March to the Lincoln Memorial and Dr. King's great "I have a dream" speech of 1963, and the championship of the Negro cause by the younger generation of today *have* effected the beginning of a reversal of this undemocratic policy we have all lived with for so long. (Funny, people never said having special schools for the *Negro* was undemocratic.) But now anyone, like psychology professor Herrnstein of Harvard, who concludes that intelligence is largely influenced by genetic factors is apt to be called a racist, whether he is or not. Professor Herrnstein's *Atlantic* article, "IQ," said nothing about the intelligence of any race, but merely confirmed Jensen's estimate that intelligence is largely (80 percent) hereditary. Nevertheless he was subjected to personal abuse and threatened with disruption of his classes, whereupon 109 Harvard and Radcliffe professors issued a statement in his defense—the battle *is* bitter!

Far too many words have been wasted on this controversy already. No knowledgeable person disputes that there are many individuals of extremely high intelligence and genius among black people both in Africa and in the United States, in history and on the contemporary scene. Christopher Jencks recently made case records of 12 Negro children with Binet IQs between 170 and 200; 180 is one in a million. In order to support the premise that Negroes are *genetically* inferior in intelligence to Caucasians, we'd have to come up with the logical conclusion that *these* blacks must be white! Which is as ridiculous as if we concluded that pure white people of low intelligence must be black.

It would be more reasonable to conclude that *even granted,* as the studies show, that intelligence is 80 percent hereditary and only 20 percent developed or inhibited by environmental factors, we can still explain an average 15 percent of "IQ inferiority" in children whose *environments* have been inferior. In fact, given physical, psychological (the "self-image") and social and cultural advantages which could *develop* the potential of a child (black or white) who lives in a well-to-do professional or business community by 20 percent, and given physical and psychological disadvantages and a different cultural background which could *inhibit* the development of a child who lives in the ghetto, we could have a *40 percent* spread, allowing for my somewhat creative female logic!

What attention, then, can we give the gifted and talented in all our communities? How can these gifted minds be developed not only to serve our society but to improve it? We can't do anything (yet, anyway) about a child's genes. We *can* do something about his environment—which includes, above everything except a very good or a very bad home, his education.

Education is in the vanguard of any attempt at permanent improvement of the environment. Urban renewal projects can raze tenements and substitute new buildings; social welfare projects can improve nutrition and living conditions; a Job Corps can find jobs. But none of these in itself can change or develop the person who lives in that environment, the person who will eventually revert to the ghetto if he does not change. Education should do that.

But does it?

It might be well to say what we mean—and do not mean—by education. We don't mean merely teachers and schools; we mean good teachers and good schools. And we can't exclude, for example, a religious or social worker who in fact teaches the people he or she is trying to help; that's education too, provided it *does* help, change, develop. Parents, it goes without saying, can be the prime educators, but above all, we can no longer leave out *the child himself*. Education is not something that is done to a child; it is something he himself accomplishes.

"You know, I learned something from my own thoughts," one child told his teacher in tremendous excitement.

Too many of us have accepted the word "education" at face value for too long. Anything—including some pretty awful things —that has been offered to us in the name of education we have patiently submitted to since we were five or six years old. And then, after submitting to it for twenty years or so, we—*some*times not so patiently—submitted our children to it.

The children who have suffered most are the gifted, whether they are the gifted on top of the hill or the gifted in the ghetto. When it comes to this important part of a child's environment— the school he goes to every day until he becomes an adult—both of these children have been "deprived," and still are being deprived, of the opportunity to learn anywhere near as much as they are capable of learning.

Worse than that, the rapidly increasing number of critics of authoritarian, lockstep, rote-memory schooling agree that gifted children not only don't learn as much as they could in such schools, they are actually deprived of learning, held back. One study which supports this thesis has been conducted by the San Diego Unified School District in cooperation with the University of California at San Diego. Results show that gifted high school graduates achieve college marks not significantly different from those of less gifted college students. It would appear they have *learned not to learn*.

When this happens, we may lose not only the benefits of these superior intellects; too often the frustration of such a student leads him to a questioning of values, sometimes to the ultimate rejection of good. He may "drop out" of society altogether, or he may attempt to destroy it. Remember, he may be one in a million, but throughout history it has been the ones, not the millions, who have changed the course of events for good or evil.

It is no use to pretend, as so many people do, that such a person doesn't exist. They exist—and it is estimated that there are about 1.5 million of them in school in the United States right now. That's just the highly gifted that we know about. There are millions more gifted children, identified and unidentified, in every city and town and school in our coutry.

And who would have it any other way?

Much has been said in schools of education for years about motivation of learning. But in practice, what happens? Grades are given, which results in the student being motivated to get a good grade; any learning he does is incidental. Bells ring at automatic intervals. How can any high school student get interested in learning 45 or 50 minutes worth of biology followed by the same amount of French followed by a mad dash to the lockers to dress for physical education, and then a mad dash back with wet hair to a measured segment of algebra?

This is the *environment* our gifted boys and girls are forced to spend most of their childhood and adolescence in. If they are very fortunate in their parents, it may be enriched by home and travel experiences, but family life is not exactly on the upgrade. For the many parents who do want to help their intellectually-needy children, though, suggestions will be found in Chapter 7.

Most children come to school at five eagerly, full of questions, smart little kids who have already taught themselves—"gifted" or not—how to walk and to talk. This is one reason why I'm sure there are many more gifted children than we officially recognize, or perhaps *could* develop through "early childhood education," as its proponents claim.

School should certainly not be an end to learning.

Yet they say children go into elementary school as question marks and come out as periods.

I can still remember the disappointed face of my five-year-old son David, when he came home from his first day of school.

"They didn't *teach* me anything," he said.

You might say he expected too much—the first day—but two years ago, when he got his Ph.D., he gave a big sigh of relief and said, "I've hated school ever since I was six."

He was one of the lucky ones; he didn't drop out.

If we could make one improvement—one only—in the environment of both advantaged and disadvantaged gifted and talented or creative children, it would be to give them a school they couldn't wait to go to every morning, a school where they could find happiness in the pursuit their special gifts have fitted them for: learning.

5

"Since When Was Genius Found Respectable?"

E. B. Browning
Aurora Leigh

SENECA (First century Roman philosopher): *There is no great genius without some touch of madness.*

RUTH STRANG (1960): *Contrary to popular opinion, the number of insane geniuses is relatively small.*

LETA HOLLINGWORTH (psychometrist at hospitals, reformatories and prisons who later specialized in the study of highly gifted children, 1942): *. . . to hear of the tremendous differences between the dullest and most intelligent individual . . . is extremely tedious to the average American listener. This is only too well-known to one who has long tried to interest foundations . . . in the education of gifted children. There is an apparent preference among donors for studying the needs and supporting the welfare of the weak, the vicious and the incompetent, and a negative disregard of the highly intelligent, leaving them to "shift for themselves."*

JOHN STUART MILL (19th-century English philosopher and economist who began to study Greek at age three and mastered Latin, classical literature, logic, political economy, history and mathematics by fourteen): *There is always need of persons . . . to discover new truths, and point out when what were once truths are true no longer. . . . there are but few persons whose experiments, if adopted by others, would be likely to be any improvement on established practice. But these few are the salt of the earth.*

GEORGE BERNARD SHAW (1923): *It is not so easy for mental giants who neither hate nor intend to injure their fellows to realize that nevertheless their fellows hate mental giants and would like to destroy them.* [St. Joan]

LETA HOLLINGWORTH (1942): *. . . there are, of course, a majority who are kindly and understanding and helpful, but it is a melancholy fact that there are also malicious and jealous people who are likely to persecute those who are formally identified as being unusual . . . even their instructors, who have felt the impulse to "take them down a peg."*

JOHN STUART MILL: *I insist . . . emphatically on the importance of genius . . . being well aware that no one will deny it in theory, but knowing also that almost everyone, in reality, is totally indifferent to it.*

PIERRE LECOMTE DU NOÜY (in *Human Destiny,* 1947): *Only a very small proportion of the population of a country—certainly less than one percent—makes a significant contribution to art, thought, culture, industry, everything which in our eyes constitutes the glory of civilization.*

JAMES J. GALLAGHER (professor and writer on gifted education, 1959): *. . . there is a general tendency to call anything that is different "unhealthy." The child who is interested in atomic physics rather than baseball is thought to be queer.*

LOUISE BATES AMES (1967): *The very bright child often needs help in being a more normal, well-rounded human being.*

LEWIS TERMAN AND MELITA ODEN (1947): *A battery of seven character tests showed gifted children above average on every one.*

As compared with unselected children they are less inclined to boast or overstate their knowledge; they are more trustworthy when under temptation to cheat; their reading preferences, character preferences, and social attitudes are more wholesome; and they score higher in emotional stability.

JAMES J. GALLAGHER (1959): *If anything, gifted children, as a group, are more emotionally stable, less tense, and more able to handle personal problems than average-ability children. This does not mean that you will not encounter emotionally disturbed gifted children.*

RICHMOND BARBOUR (educator and journalist, Assistant Superintendent of Schools and a leader in gifted education in San Diego for many years; in an interview, 1972): *In the late 1940's we made a series of studies which showed that a disproportionate number of gifted children [IQ 148 and over] were having problems, or were social misfits. When we put them in special programs designed to fill their needs, a large number of these problems disappeared.*

"This is the first time, this year, in my whole life, I wasn't considered weird for reading Camus, Sartre, Freud and anything. Furthermore others were reading the same things and we could sit around and discuss them."

This student opinion of a special program for the gifted at Pt. Loma High School in San Diego, California, is one of the best expressions of the need for such programs as well as of the feelings of the gifted student himself that I know of. It's included in a dissertation by two of the three young men who worked out the program; they tested it, and then wrote up an evaluation for their Ph.D.'s from the United States International University's Graduate School of Leadership and Human Behavior, in June 1969.

Dr. David C. Wright is Director of Exceptional Child Services, and Dr. David P. Hermanson, one of the original teachers at

Pt. Loma, is now Coordinator of Secondary Gifted Programs in the San Diego City Schools. As the eighth-largest school district in the nation, San Diego can offer more to its over 7000 identified gifted students than is possible in small districts, of course, with only a few. But the principle behind the innovative Independent Study Unit—a "school within a school" for a selection of gifted, "homogeneous," students—is still under fierce debate: see Chapter 8, "Should Pupils Be Grouped By Ability?"

It would seem reasonable to listen to the point of view of the gifted themselves, at the high school level where their mental ages have reached or exceeded those of many of the adults who have the say about how those brilliant minds are to be developed. This is not to say that even the most gifted don't have anything to learn, still, from adults. They do, and most of them wouldn't want the responsibilities and tedious jobs that go along with administering their educations.

Still, one of the most important things I have to say in this book is that we should *listen* to gifted youth. They have original ideas that are brushed aside, not even considered, for the solution of some of our greatest contemporary problems. And they have the energy, the time, and the brains to work on those solutions if we'll only let them, instead of wasting the most creative years of their lives in rote-memory of out-of-date facts, which they have to learn in order to get into college—which may not yet offer much more.

It isn't hard to understand, if you think about it, why some brilliant students drop out of such schools. But as dropouts, society has no use for them at all.

Yet even small children in elementary school can help solve community problems. Robert Oppenheimer, the physicist, says there are small children playing in the street who could solve some of his top problems because they have ways of seeing things that an adult has lost. And Edmund Bacon, the head of a town planning commission in Philadelphia, actually used elementary school boys and girls; he got them to study and discuss the plans with their parents and other adults, and to study the community itself. They came up with some of the best solutions!

Neil Postman and Charles Weingartner suggested that high school students could form themselves into teams of ten or twelve with a teacher and a community member to study such problems as traffic control, crime, strikes, race relations, urban blight, drug addiction, garbage disposal or air pollution, with the idea of "inventing authentic solutions." So many of today's students express nothing but scorn for the old "student government" idea; they consider it merely a token delegation of authority which is meaningless. They feel they are capable of a more realistic use of their ideas and skills.

When I walked into Morse High School's Independent Studies Center, I dropped right into the middle of a session that proves the point. Mel Zeddies, their teacher, had invited a new member of the Board of Education to "rap" with his seventeen kids in the faculty lounge at lunchtime. The students asked a series of rapid fire questions about education, and came up with some "far-out" suggestions which no one paid much attention to. *But it might be a good idea if we did,* I thought.

For instance, San Diego has a serious classroom problem based on a legislative decision (the Field Act) that outlaws as earthquake hazards schools built before 1935. Since San Diegans have been using such schools, they've suddenly found it necessary to replace several at once; the taxpayers are already bleeding from constantly rising property levies, and besides, they *like* those old schools—they went to them!

This was just one of the problems the kids discussed, for starters. One boy suggested that since large apartment construction is creating a need for new schools in their area, the builders should contribute to the construction. (This was not an original idea; it has been mentioned in the newspapers.)

"They are contributing park land for recreation," the Board Member pointed out. "A school might be asking too much."

"What do you think about free schools?" a girl named Kellie asked. "Why couldn't the apartment owners just put up a small building in the park? And have a free school?"

As often happens with creative people, she didn't *say* all that she saw in her own mind, and she had already asked so many questions that the Board member laughed and said he'd better give someone else a chance; so that was the end of that teenage solution to one of the top problems in many communities today.

But *I* can see it: a small, simple, "open" school building in a park, for the children who live all around it; a sort of "free school" but with the School District behind it; the building paid for by men who could afford to build a great many much larger and more elaborate apartment units. They offer tennis courts, golf courses, playgrounds and swimming pools—why not an elementary school? And perhaps a "middle school" too? Modern "schools without walls" would be comparatively inexpensive, if built along with the apartments, and could be furnished and staffed by the school district.

But nobody listens to kids.

After lunch Kim, Terry, Ada and some of the others took me to see their special room, which has to be the most *colorful* classroom in the world!

The most dazzling feature is their own individual partitioned-off study desks (carrels) which each student has plastered with gaudily designed wallpaper and other bright decorations. There's a frieze around the ceiling painted by Mike Stewart, who is also doing an imaginative mural (with everybody's help in the execution) called "Departure of the Spirits." I can tell already, from the beginnings of a splendid, rearing horse, that it's going to be a work of art.

"I like to draw animals," Mike says. "I read all the books I can get about them, and watch them at the zoo and anywhere."

An inescapable impression you get is that these kids are proud of each other. Caroline, a serious-minded and sedate Negro who makes wise remarks in very few words, admires Kellie (the girl of many words!) for her unconventional ideas. Somebody tells me Annie O'Quinn is great in Speech and Drama, and a couple of others say I must read Maria's poetry. From the sheaf of it they show me I'd say she's one up on Wordsworth already, and it's good.

Kim Leavitt puts out a newspaper for the group, and plans to write a book called *The Education Machine.* "I like to think up titles," he says, and shows me a poem he wrote called "Technology's Child."

There's an old bathtub in one corner of the room which the kids plan to use for experiments in marine biology, and another corner is partitioned off by bookshelves into a lounge for reading on a comfortable couch and rocking chair, or for small-group meetings. There are heaps of books not only on the shelves but all over the room.

The City Gifted Program provides funds for books, some to the students themselves, and Dr. Zeddies has bought heaps of paperbacks which Rex, their friend and T. A., is busy cataloging. Even more important to Mel Zeddies, perhaps, are the two computers he managed to acquire for his kids.

Morse High School is currently under fire as a racially imbalanced school, preponderantly black, but its Independent Study Center, including black, brown, white and Oriental boys and girls, all chosen for their exceptional mental ability, might well be a model for all schools as far as racial mixture is concerned. And this, I feel sure their gentle, scholarly teacher believes, is even more important than those computers he wangled for them.

At another I. S. Center, at Clairemont High School, I found a long, narrow room with several seminar-type tables. A variety of activities were going on, some so noisy that other groups had to say "Knock it off, will you?" At one of the tables Cecil Munsey, District Resource Teacher, was showing the new editor of their I. S. newspaper how to do headlines; afterwards he asked me to give an informal seminar on feature article writing, to which anybody who wanted could come.

I recognized an old friend of mine at another table—the French wife of a history professor at San Diego State; she comes in weekly to give French lessons, so the kids can go as fast as they want to in the language. An art teacher comes in, too, for five hours every Friday, for the same purpose: to give individualized instruction at a gifted level.

When Mr. Munsey introduced the two master teachers, Mr. Haas and Mr. Grove, he said, "The one with the beard is the conservative and the one with short hair is the radical." They both laughed.

Jim Grove, the "conservative," teaches Honors English, and still believes in the good old classroom lecture. Bob Haas, the scientist on the team, is quietly enthusiastic about the concept of independent inquiry.

"This room is full of undiscovered talent," he told me.

All over the United States, such "independent study" plans differ, as do San Diego's five high school centers. The nature of independent study itself, school facilities and personnel, and the needs of the unique students require differing plans, and besides this kind of education is new and rare in the public schools. Problems of administration and financing must be solved, and only experience with trial plans can develop the solutions.

At some "schools within schools" it's possible for gifted students to spend the whole day with their master teachers, covering the necessary subject matter for graduation in individually designed and group units, or studying on their own and taking "challenge tests" to prove they have mastered the material. They are given much free time—at school or elsewhere—to "do their own thing," and the enthusiasm engendered by this freedom to follow their interests leads to a great deal more learning than they would get in the traditional class. They demonstrate this by in-depth, scholarly papers, scientific experiments, playwriting and production, filmmaking and in many other creative ways. Students who don't measure up just don't stay in the program.

At La Jolla's highly regarded center, in an older high school building, the kids have two rooms, in addition to a small office for the teachers, Mrs. Betty Morrison and Dave Vigilante (in the absence of their original team teacher, Tim Tanzer, who spent half the year 1972 studying gifted education in England). One room is a small amphitheater for unit lectures and discussion and—when there are no classes—for talking. The other, with individual desks, is the quiet room, which is something Morse High could certainly use!

The Independent Study Center at Crawford High has been

both highly praised and criticized for its more conservative approach. The teachers, Paul Wright and Sally Remington, and counselor Florence Evans, are outstanding, and a copy of the 1971–72 evaluation of their program is being printed by the San Diego City Schools as a valuable appraisal of this type of gifted education. Interested educators may be able to obtain a copy by request from Dr. David P. Hermanson, Coordinator of Secondary Gifted Programs at 6404 Linda Vista Road, San Diego, Ca. 92111.

All the involved students, parents, administrators and teachers are enthusiastic; the chief problem is to placate those who are not involved, of course. The hope is that these gifted pioneers will blaze the trail to freedom in education for all students—and teachers.

The Report to Congress states, and I have observed in my visits to some of the schools, that identification of the gifted is hampered by apathy and even hostility among teachers, administrators, guidance counselors and psychologists.

"Up to last year we couldn't even mention the word *gifted*," said an elementary school teacher who had had a "cluster" class for several years. "But I think it's finally getting more respectable."

The elementary cluster class includes gifted children transported from surrounding schools (usually by their parents) at a central school, and includes nongifted students as well. One of its most appreciated benefits, according to parents, is the opportunity for their children to make friends with other gifted children; this is especially important for the rare "genius-type kid."

"There is an enormous individual and social cost when talent among the nation's children and youth goes undiscovered and undeveloped," the Report to Congress states, along with overwhelming evidence from all parts of the country that this talent is not being developed.

For instance, there is a great need for multilingual people in order to achieve a closer understanding among nations and our number one goal of world peace, yet many high schools are offering *less* language than they did thirty years ago—before the atom was split!

Why? I met gifted students at the Independent Studies Centers who are fascinated by languages—not just one or two, which is all any student can fit into a traditional high school curriculum, but *all* languages.

Craig Jackson is one of the "language nuts" I've run into this year. He takes third year French, fourth year German (after winning a national German contest that sent him to Germany last summer) and, in Independent Studies, he's taking Russian.

I love the surprising answers you get when you ask gifted kids questions. "What's the most interesting thing about language?" I asked Craig.

"Grammar," he said. (!!!!) "And I like to look at all languages, and compare the ways of expressing thoughts in different languages."

And I asked him, "What's your favorite language?"

"English."

And, "Do you plan to be a linguist? Teach?"

"I'd like to see what college has to offer before I decide— maybe something in science," he said, "or I might like anthropology if I knew more about it." Languages are useful, of course, in any field.

On a field trip to the Pt. Loma tide pools with another high school group, I sat on the rocks by the ocean and talked to a boy named Tim. Expecting the unusual by now, I got it.

He likes politics—started campaigning at thirteen, when he founded a Youth for Nixon Club—and writes political satire. He goes to the summer Tar Camps, which I gathered are like the Student Congresses I used to take my Speech students to, where they write their own bills and run mock legislatures.

"I lined up some speaking engagements for one of the local candidates last year at school," he said, "and he didn't come! But frustrations are a part of politics; that's one thing you have to learn."

He quoted from John C. Calhoun on what's the most important thing in politics: "Get elected."

We laughed. He didn't mind talking to a strange adult while a boy and girl called to him "See the narwhal," and he kidded back, "If you've seen one narwhal you've seen 'em all," and a girl with a remarkable set of values found a smooth pinkish rock shaped exactly like a heart, but threw it back into the ocean because the Pt. Loma tide pools are a restricted area—you can't take anything away.

"What else do you like?" I asked Tim.

"I taught myself German, on my own, after a little Spanish in the sixth grade, and I had two years of Latin in junior high." He went on to mention Arabic, Italian, Japanese, Greek, Portuguese and Russian—in that order—and "the history of linguistic concepts."

His favorite language is Esperanto! He can speak and write it, thinks it's the most euphonious language, and told me it was invented in 1887 by Dr. Ludovic Zamenhof, a Pole.

"I hadn't heard anything about it since I was in college," I confessed.

"There are ten million in the movement now," he assured me, and before our ten minutes or so of conversation was over I knew he also likes astronomy, hates math (except sidereal) and is not looking forward to college because of the social life.

"Don't you have to have a lot of socializing in politics?" I asked.

"That's the part I don't like," he admitted.

Their teacher, Mike Lorch, the original science man of the pilot Independent Studies program at Pt. Loma High, was pointing out and explaining the levels of rock structure which tell its age, and answering questions about marine life in the tide pools. I got to talking to the other teacher on the team, Mr. Fristrom, who specializes in the humanities, and I mentioned Tim's reluctance about college social life.

He said, "Tim's come a long way. We found him hidden in remedial classes and the corners of regular rooms." And he told me about another girl who is shy; he says Independent Studies is helping her but so far she is just doing "small things"—"not big things like Tim, but significant for her." They're relating other things to her interest in art.

What a magnificent classroom—the vast, sparkling Pacific on a sunny gold day, two teachers who know their fields well enough to answer the sharp questions of the gifted (or most of them!) and the boys and girls themselves, laughing, sliding down the ancient rocks and peering into the tidepools to learn about life under the sea.

Mr. Lorch has obtained funds for lab equipment for his "school within a school" and calls it "the beginning of a laboratory for the gifted." Professor Gowan says the schools of the future will consist of laboratories and libraries—what a delight!

I think the two boys I overheard on the rocks saying "He's a real philosopher besides being a scientist" must have been referring to Mr. Lorch.

At another Independent Study Center I talked to a senior named Dick, whose chief interest was another surprise.

"I like education," he said enthusiastically. "I read Jerome Bruner's *Process of Education* when I was a sophomore, and I wanted to get into Independent Studies but they wouldn't take me. They called me an underachiever, so I read 26 books and wrote reports and term papers on education and got into the I.S. program at the end of my junior year."

He likes John Holt's books, and is working on a science project on ESP.

Women's Liberationists will be pleased to hear that the only two 2-time winners of high school sweepstakes in San Diego Science Fair history were both girls: one was red-haired Tamzon Feeney who was also one of the best actresses I ever had in Drama at the Academy of our Lady of Peace; the other, Maureen King, was the oldest of a large family, whose first prizewinning entry at Clairemont High was "A Study of the Developmental Enzyme Patterns of Genetically Obese Mice"!! She won a trip to the International Science Fair in Kansas City during her junior year in high school. There she won a second place award, and then spent the summer at the Jackson Laboratory in Bar Harbor, Maine, on a scholarship from the National Science Foundation.

These are just a handful of the "identified" gifted students in one city. I wish I had room for more. If you want to read a delightful book about one genius, I recommend Audrey Grost's *Genius in Residence;* and for interesting details about 400 of the most outstanding men and women of the twentieth century, see Victor and Mildred Goertzel's *Cradles of Eminence.*

What happens to bright children in the many schools all over the country which make no provision for their extraordinary eagerness to learn? How can the discussion of such children be "tedious"? It's hard to understand our great national inability or refusal to appreciate intellectual achievement and hard to forgive, for it causes a constant strain on the resolution of good students to excel in their work. "Peer" pressure to be "just like everybody else" tempts many junior high and high school boys and girls to hide or minimize their talents; surprisingly, twice as many boys as girls become "underachievers," Yet girls are often unwilling to seem smarter than the big thing in their lives at that age—boys! Women's Lib may change that attitude, but it hasn't yet.

"I wonder how many people think we are weird?" one of the I.S. girls asked another at Pt. Loma.

"We *are* weird," she laughed.

But "we" was the word that mattered. Good students need friends who understand them, and enjoy the same things.

Although many studies show gifted students to be if anything less emotionally unstable than the general population, they are sensitive human beings, with feelings that can be hurt just like anyone else's. They want to be liked.

Some of them are snobs; so are many people with average IQs. Some are black, some are white, some are short, some are tall, some are kind, some are mean, some are graceful, some are awkward, some are tactful, some are not.

The only difference between talented and other individuals lies in the talent itself, and *that* is relative. No matter how good you are at anything—tennis, singing, mathematics or writing poetry, there's always someone who's better (or will be next year), and even if you get to be number one champion in the world at one thing, look at all the other championships you don't come anywhere near.

Considering the attitude of so many people toward the gifted, it's really a wonder more geniuses don't turn to evil pursuits. But this is not what happens. One of their outstanding general characteristics is their high moral standards and concern about social problems, which is fortunate for society.

Albert Schweitzer is the personification of this trait. He said, "Whatever you have received more than others in health, in talents, in ability, in success . . . you must render in return an unusually great sacrifice of your life for other life."

A junior high school girl, Deborah Krolik, expressed this feeling in a Quarter Report for Mrs. Jodie Bruhn, whose outstanding gifted program at Hale Junior High includes social service at a nearby school for the handicapped.

"My experiences at Sunshine School have been so numerous, pleasant, and enjoyable, that it is hard to put into words my eagerness of going there each morning. . . . I suppose . . . the most important thing I have learned is that I have found my goal in life—teaching handicapped children. The smallest bit of progress or eagerness displayed by the children fills me with a wonderful sense of achievement. Little words and actions expressing emotions and feelings are most important to me—a smile, a hug, a greeting, a proud voice saying 'Look what I've made!' . . . ."

In the past, children like these have managed to sit through twelve or thirteen years of monotonous schooling and still become great social, intellectual, scientific and industrial leaders. But let's see, in the next chapter, what that is like for the children.

6
Are Bright Children Bored in Our Schools?

MARIA MONTESSORI (1912): *. . . in . . . the public schools . . . the children are repressed in the spontaneous expression of their personality till they are almost like dead beings. In such a school the children, like butterflies mounted on pins, are fastened each to his place, the desk, spreading the useless wings of barren and meaningless knowledge which they have acquired.*

ALBERT EINSTEIN (quoted in *Einstein,* ed Paul Schlipp, 1951): *It is in fact nothing short of a miracle that the modern methods of instruction have not yet entirely strangled the holy curiosity of inquiry.*

SENATOR JACOB JAVITS (in the *Congressional Record,* Jan. 28, 1969): *The talented child has often been the forgotten child and the underachiever despite his extraordinary potential because he becomes bored with unchallenging programs.*

LOUISE BATES AMES (1967): *The bright child is seldom bored in school.*

JOHN HOLT (1970): *Almost all children are bored in school. Why shouldn't they be? We would be.*

JAMES BRYANT CONANT (1959): *In all but a few of the schools I have visited* [he personally visited one-half of over 100 high schools in 26 states for this study] *the majority of the bright boys and girls were not working hard enough.*

HERBERT KOHL (teacher and writer, 1967): *How can the children be expected to be alert, curious, and excited when the teacher is so often bored?*

ALVIN I. EURICH (educator and writer on educational reform, 1969): *Many behavior problems disappear when children are challenged intellectually.*

GEORGE I. THOMAS AND JOSEPH CRESCIMBENI (1966): *Many gifted pupils are enthusiastic about school, but others are not, as is evidenced by their failure to go on to college or to complete high school.*

STEPHEN NYMAN (a New Jersey high school underground newspaper journalist, 1970): *What is palmed off as an education is largely a collection of fact and information, a collection of required readings and required subjects that have no meaning to our lives. Physics, French, U.S. History, English all being taught (with emphasis on the teaching not the learning) to get people into college, to complete requirements, to proliferate lies; being taught because they "have" to be taught, and being taught not to help us cope with and try to save the dying world we will have to take over or to help us cope with and save each other, but because they are on a list of "available subjects." The rationale of schools being a place where facts are transferred can no longer be accepted in a world where facts multiply every few years. . . . The approach is only a century outmoded.* [See John Birmingham, ed.]

MARK VAN DOREN (Poet and professor): *Freedom to use the mind is the greatest happiness.*

GEORGE LEONARD (journalist, 1968): *Education, at best, is ecstatic.*

HEIDI MARTIN (a seventh grader, 1972):
> *Tests*
> *Teachers, Friday*
> *Throw up, die, dead.*
> *Why?*
> *BOO!!!!!*

"Well, now, take my courses as an example, I've had the courses in junior high school. We read one chapter a week, complete one work sheet a week, and have a movie on Friday. The instructor is so lazy that I run the projector and we even exchange tests for correction which are true-false types. It's a bore, waste of time, but if I don't play the game I won't get into college."

This high school student's opinion, taped in 1968 for the Hermanson and Wright dissertation, contrasts sharply with that of the boy who started off so eagerly, "This is the first time, in my whole life, I wasn't considered weird for reading Camus, Sartre, Freud. . . ."

The problem of boredom is especially critical for the highly gifted. Champions of education for the gifted rarely make any distinction, but when possible we should. (There is as much difference between 140 and 180 as there is between 100 and 140.) Studies have shown that while among the total gifted population, emotional and behavior problems are no more common or indeed less common than in the general population, among the few with extremely high IQs, there may be more cases of maladjustment, and this is not surprising.

In a high school honors math class, my daughter sat next to a boy who never did any homework and composed music in his notebook while the rest of the class tackled the difficult problems their teacher liked to bring in for them. Sometimes, Frea said, "when we all got stuck, including the teacher, Tom would look up and straighten us out."

This boy got a C in math, along with poor grades in other subjects, because he didn't do the work; with that scholastic average he didn't go to college. "I don't think he even wanted to," Frea said. "He was a nice-looking, normal type of boy but he never had any friends or participated in anything but the band for a while. He never made any trouble; he just didn't care."

When the Bank of America awards were given to the seniors, Frea was as surprised as we were when she got the one in math.

"A boy like Tom ought to get that," she said.

We wonder what happened to him, and if there's still a chance he may use that fantastic mathematical ability. How many of the few who have it become Einsteins and Norbert Wieners? How many others are lost because they sit alone in a large (or small) high school, with no one to talk to because no one can speak their language? Since genius IQ may be one in a million, there aren't likely to be two around!

Four hundred outstanding men and women of the twentieth century, many of whom were geniuses, were included in Victor and Mildred Goertzel's *Cradles of Eminence,* which contained such names as Jane Addams, the Barrymores, Alexander Graham Bell, Enrico Caruso, George Washington Carver, Cézanne, Charles Chaplin, Winston Churchill, Freud, Hitler, Ibsen, Helen Keller, John D. Rockefeller and Woodrow Wilson, at random mention. Three out of five of these 400 "loathed" school (the classroom); this was an "international phenomenon," however—not just one confined to the United States. Grieg, the composer, stood under a rainspout so his teacher would send him home; Sigrid Undset "hated school intensely"; William Saroyan said he "resented school, but never resented learning."

The enthusiasm with which gifted children and gifted parents (but not always the parents who are not gifted themselves) seize upon special programs such as independent study and individualized instruction indicates that Saroyan's attitude is that of most exceptionally intelligent students. So is the fact that these boys and girls, though bored in school, often read avidly in books supposedly far too "difficult" for their age group. (I was a good little girl, ordinarily, but *I sneaked books out of the adult section of the library!*)

Besides being bored in school, and often *because* they were, many of the outstanding 400 were also considered stupid. Thomas Edison said he was always at the foot of his class! And Albert Einstein was considered dull by both his teachers and his parents. Rachmaninoff changed poor grades (1s) on his report card to good ones (4s) at a Conservatory of Music. Pablo Picasso refused to do anything at school but paint, so it's less surprising that he didn't do well; what surprised everyone was that he had no trouble in passing difficult entrance examinations for higher education. This was true of a number of other geniuses who did poorly in school.

Besides reading on their own, many of these children were taught by their parents. There was no parent-tutored boy or girl among the Four Hundred who was not grateful for the experience, the authors said.

When our youngest son became ill, at eleven, we taught him at home. I was supposed to be teaching him "the seventh grade," and his principal gave me all the standard textbooks. But the doctors had told us that Johnny had an incurable disease, so we wanted him to learn everything he could learn, in the "fifteen months" they said he might have.

That's why I didn't bother much about the textbooks. He took one look at the seventh grade math and said disappointedly, "There's nothing new."

Since he had had an outstanding young man teacher in the sixth grade who gave him some advanced math I didn't even understand, I wasn't much help in that line, but we let him do algebra.

"The high schools don't like us to start algebra in junior high," the principal told us, "because it's supposed to be taught in high school."

But Johnny was doing all the seventh grade review problems with no errors, so the principal gave us the eighth grade book; that had a few new odds and ends but still no algebra. I sometimes wonder, when it comes to bright children, if we really need a junior high school at all. Perhaps the answer is to use it as a catching-up place for children who have not yet learned to read well and who need the review in arithmetic, with some time for "fun subjects." Those who didn't need the review could then go from elementary school to a four year high school. I can just hear the Education Establishment exploding at such an idea; never mind, it's just one of those creative brainstorms. It is true, however, that no one can ever quite decide what to do with junior high. Boys and girls in the same city may go from eighth grade to freshman year in high school or from ninth grade to the sophomore year. The new idea of middle schools has run into even more confusion—shall the middle school cover fifth grade? ninth grade?

At the end of Johnny's year at home, although he had worked only a few hours a day at his leisure, instead of from 8 to 3, and with a teacher who had to do little more than make suggestions, Johnny was invited to graduate with the eighth grade class. Possibly the compassionate principal just felt that he would like to graduate, although the decision was based on achievement tests with a battery median in the tenth grade (10.2), ranging from 7.6 in science (a neglected area in our family background) to 12.3 in study skills, and eleventh-grade math.

But by this time Johnny had achieved a remission from his disease which was to last nearly four years; it gave him the chance to join his older brother on the high school tennis team, to get three varsity letters and to win the Harvard award for most outstanding boy in his junior class. He was a senior, and had just won a state scholarship to the college of his choice on the basis of his college entrance exam scores when the medicine finally stopped working.

He had said, "I want to do every single thing that I can do." And he had. He hadn't wasted any of his precious time.

In teaching him this way, not worrying about the conventions as most parents, teachers and administrators feel they must, I came to a few conclusions about why school is "boring" for so many children.

It is not usually the teacher's fault so much as it is the system she or he is forced to conform to. Even a great teacher is hand-cuffed by administrative rules (if she has a "nonsupportive" prin-cipal) and by the material she has to "cover" (the textbook, no matter how colorful, with its standardized "things to learn"). (An extremely interesting book about texts is Hillel Black's *The American Schoolbook,* William Morrow Company, 1967.) Johnny dutifully did the exercises at the end of each chapter in his social studies book, but he hated it—until I let him loose in the ency-clopedia and any other books in the house or at the library on the same general subject as The Chapter. *Then* he got interested, be-cause *there was no end* to what he could find out about—China, for instance; China is a fascinating subject, but not when all you know about it is the capital, imports and exports and a few other odds and ends, which get mixed up with the capitals, imports and exports of a bunch of other countries at the same time.

So we decided he'd done enough exercises, and could just skim through the book and pick out the things he wanted to know more about. This resulted, of course, in his knowing more geography and history than his classmates at school ever learned. And since we also dispensed with memorizing facts for tests, which he'd forget as soon as the tests were taken, he could use that wasted rote-memory time to find out many more details which he did remember because they interested him.

Another stupid thing which I had been doing for years, even in teaching college Freshman Composition, was the assignment of "theme topics." Teachers and textbook writers have been figuring out lockstep composition subjects without thinking about it simply because this is the way it's always been done! The subjects seldom fit any of the students, let alone all of them. With ingenuity, a good student can twist them around to "where he's at," but most students just sigh and hammer it out. The results are nearly al-ways wordy, say-nothing pages which bore both writer and reader. English teachers assign these papers, I suppose, in order to have something to correct the spelling and punctuation of!

I decided not to do this to Johnny, even though it was what the

English curriculum prescribed. Perhaps it takes a very special reason to give you the courage to break the rules, but all teachers should start realizing that *every child who is bored in school* is a special reason to do something about it. Teachers like Jonathan Kozol (*Death at an Early Age*) in the Boston schools and James Herndon (*The Way It Spozed to Be*) in San Francisco had the courage, and succeeded in teaching children who had never learned before; but they were fired for not conforming to the pattern which has been boring most of us since we were in the first grade.

"Write anything you want to," I told Johnny, "but write one page in your composition book every day."

"What'll I write about?" he asked, as any class would if a teacher suddenly took away her support.

"Look out the window and write what you see. Write what you're thinking—"

"Like, 'This is a stupid assignment,' " he said, grinning.

"Absolutely," I told him. "Be honest. That's the only way you'll write anything original. Otherwise you just copy down what you're supposed to think, somebody else's ideas."

I'm not sure these were my exact words—this was more than ten years ago—but I am sure of what Johnny wrote, because I still have his fifteen-cent composition book.

He wrote narratives about a camping trip and a train trip, several descriptions of landscapes ("out the window"), some criticisms of TV shows and books he read, some suggestions for educational innovations (!), a couple of poems, considerable sports-reporting on World Series and football games, some letters to his brother-in-law in the Air Force (when I said that would count), and then about half-way through the notebook he started writing *stories*—and stopped confining himself to a page a day. He let loose with his imagination and the first ones were pretty wild, but they got better and better.

The last one was a satire on Westerns, "Show Down at Gallows City," and it begins, "The saloon door opened, and in came Saloon man Sam. Counting his 2 pint hat, he was 6'6" and didn't look any too kind. Sam was a stranger in town, Gallows City that is. I want a milk! said Sam, coming to the counter. Everybody in the saloon started laughing. One man said, give the baby his milk. Sam was good-natured enough to let him off with a black eye."

I didn't "correct" his notebook, I just enjoyed it with him, but sometimes I would tell him something like, in this case, how to punctuate dialog. It's better to point out one thing at a time, rather than a hodge-podge of different errors on every piece of writing. It's more memorable—and less stuffy.

The surprising thing is, when you look it over, you see that Johnny actually did write the very things a teacher usually suggests: narrative, description, autobiography, letters, literary criticism, even book reports, sportswriting, poetry and short stories. But he did each one *when it was on his mind,* not when he had no ideas on that subject that day.

Our spelling method, which resulted in an 11.9 on the achievement tests, was very simple. I gave him a 500-word list from a college handbook, orally, and checked the ones he got wrong. Next day we went over the checked words and narrowed it down some more. Next day—and so forth. We were through with spelling by the end of the first month. I understand the current method of teaching spelling is based on rules, not lists, but I wonder if that doesn't waste some time? Of course, spelling comes easy to some people and doesn't come at all to others just as bright—or brighter. And somebody can always correct your spelling, so it really isn't all that important.

Reading and writing should be fun, and we teachers, of all people, have been taking the joy out of both. We shouldn't assign "book reports" on a limited choice of "classics," either ancient or modern, or the kids will hate books. The "Reading is FUN-damental" program, founded by Margaret McNamara in Washington, D.C. (RIF, Smithsonian Institution, Washington, D.C. 20560), operates in disadvantaged areas on the theory that a child should have the fun of picking out "a book of his own" from a large assortment of good ones, and the idea works. "Forming a child's taste" by force-feeding *our* choices (or even the same "famous" books which bored us when we were in school) is more likely to make the child dislike good books than like them.

Johnny didn't like to read (this has made the book I wrote about him popular with children who don't like to read), but when I let him read anything he wanted, he found *some* books he liked: Tolkien's books, Schulz's *Peanuts*—he had a collection of them, and made up a hilarious Peanuts Dictionary—Sinclair Lewis's *Arrowsmith,* books by tennis players and books on chess. Books can both form and reflect a child's interests.

There are so many fascinating things to learn that there is no excuse for boring children; in fact it sometimes seems as if schools go out of their way to do just that. Boredom is at the root of the dropout problem in high schools, and it isn't confined to students with low academic potential; it has been estimated that as many as half of the gifted drop out of high school and college. This doesn't mean that some of these dropouts don't achieve success—even eminence—in later life, as Dr. and Mrs. Goertzel's work shows.

But if our system of compulsory schooling is not *helping* people to achieve this success, even holding them back from their later contributions to society, then what's our excuse for making them waste so many years "getting educated"? If boys and girls who teach themselves, are tutored, or participate in innovative programs, are enjoying learning, while the majority of our teachers and/or textbooks are boring around 50 million U. S. schoolchildren including about four million mentally gifted and who knows how many creatively gifted and multi-talented kids every year, what's the point of prolonging the agony?

What are we going to do about it?

7
What Can Parents Do?

JOHN CURTIS GOWAN AND GEORGE DEMOS (1964): *The question sometimes arises as to whether parents should be told that their child is gifted. . . . Should parents be told their son has made the varsity football squad? Should they be told he has been elected Class President? . . . Should they be told he plans to go to college? The answer to all these questions is "Yes."*

LOUISE BATES AMES (1967): *If parents could think more of a high IQ as a good thing to have and less as a measure of the child's total functioning, they would be less likely to fall into the trap of pushing their children ahead in school . . . just because they are bright.*

JOHN CURTIS GOWAN (in "Twenty-Five Suggestions for Parents of Able Children," *Gifted Child Quarterly,* Vol. 8, 1964): *There's a difference between pushing and intellectual stimulation. Parents should avoid "pushing" a child into reading, "exhibiting" him before others or courting undue publicity about him. On the other hand, parents should seek in every way to stimulate and widen the child's mind, through suitable experiences in books, recreation, travel and the arts.*

ANN F. ISAACS (Editor of the *Gifted Child Quarterly,* in an article in Vol. 10, 1966, "A Survey of Suggested Preparation of Teachers of the Gifted."): *. . . some parents . . . view has been: "so that is what is wrong with my child, he is gifted!"*

A community opinion on MIKE GROST, who later graduated from

the University of Michigan, with honors, at 14): *So you're little Mike Grost? Your parents like to think you're a genius, huh?*

MIKE GROST: *No, sir. My parents prefer to think of me as a natural resource.* [This anecdote is taken from Audrey Grost's *Genius in Residence,* 1970.]

JAMES GALLAGHER (1959): *Gifted children are among our most important national resources. . . . [but] How often have you heard the following statement from parents? "Well, my Johnny is not a genius, but at least he is all right in the head."*

RUTH STRANG (1960): *Gifted children vary so widely. . . . Some need control; others need freedom. Some are overstimulated; others need to be challenged. . . . Some receive an embarrassing amount of praise and recognition; others need more outspoken appreciation.*

PAUL D. PLOWMAN AND JOSEPH P. RICE (California State Consultants in gifted education, 1969): *. . . "Successful programs" are abandoned because they are exposed to incessant pressure from teachers and parents. . . . There is clearly a need to study the social, cultural, and psychological motives of parents and teachers rejecting programs that involve unconventional approaches, risk-taking, or unusual commitment.*

JOHN CURTIS GOWAN (in "Twenty-Five Suggestions," 1964): *Support the school efforts to plan for able children. Help to interest the PTA in the problem. Support study groups on gifted children. . . . Support community action. . . .*

WILLARD ABRAHAM (1958): *For too long parents and teachers have been wary of each other, worried that the other will stand in judgment, find fault, and lack understanding. When it comes to the gifted, or any other child, neither is a* better *judge; the observation, knowledge, and cooperation of both are needed.*

An elementary school teacher in an individualized program using parents as teachers' aides (1970): *We couldn't do it without the parents.*

Dear parents of the gifted,

I've been reading *Cradles of Eminence,* a book about the perfectly awful parents of most of the famous men and women of the twentieth century; the moral seems to be that no matter how bad the parents are (or *because* they are?) genius, like murder, "will out."

What we have to realize, of course, is that the parents described in Victor and Mildred Goertzel's book were of another generation of parents, and parenthood has changed in some ways since Victorian times. Besides, many of those gifted children suffered a great deal of unhappiness, and if that is the price, do we want to pay it? Perhaps that's why the children in the ghetto may be the eminent men and women of tomorrow; perhaps pain is a prerequisite for production. But if we can, we as parents certainly want to raise *happily* gifted children.

I can't speak from experience as far as genius is concerned, but I have picked up a few ideas from raising a moderately gifted family; they may be of some help to those of you who are just beginning, or of nostalgic interest to others whose sons and daughters are growing or grown up. Also I've talked to some parents of the highly gifted for their experiences.

Soon after our first daughter, Frea, was born, I learned Rule One (in order, not in importance): don't brag about your child, or you will be very unpopular with other parents. I have to admit I didn't follow this rule without numerous exceptions for the next twenty years, while I raised four lovely, beautiful, bright, delightful daughters and sons, but anyhow I *knew* better.

"Give Mom an opening and she'll plunge right in," a teenage son once said in mingled disgust, resignation and tender indulgence.

I did, however, develop an antidote; I made it a point to say the nicest things I could think of about other people's children too. This is easy, because I like children.

There's a sort of parents'-eye-view which makes it easier to see the virtues *and* the faults in your own children than in others. When Frea was a baby I thought she had the most beautiful dimpled knees in the world, and I had a neighbor whose baby's legs looked like toothpicks. Of course I never *said* this, I just thought it. What I said was, "Sally's hair is so pretty. I wish Frea had curly hair. But I *do* like her legs."

"Oh, do you?" my neighbor sniffed. "They're so fat!"

The next rule I remember learning was when my second daughter was in the second grade. She had skipped the first because Frea, two years older, in playing school with her, had inconsiderately taught her how to read before the first grade teacher had a chance.

Sheila Mary was a chubby little girl; when she sang "I'm a little tea-pot, short and stout," she looked the part, and we thought she was adorable. But she came home from school one day with a smile which even her parents had to admit was a bit smug.

"Why did I skip a grade, Mother? Am I *very smart?*" she asked.

I reached fast for Rule Two: teach your little ones not to brag about themselves, or they will be very unpopular with other children. "Yes, honey," I said, "but you were just lucky you were born that way—it's what you do with it that counts. Don't go around bragging about it, though, or *you won't have any friends.*"

Since she was the most socially-conscious child in our family anyway, I never had to say any more. In fact, I've wondered since if I should have laid it on so thick, because this leads up to Rule Three, which is probably the most important. As parents (particularly of *highly* gifted children) *you must not be too concerned about what other people think, and you must teach your child not to be too concerned about that either.*

If this seems to be a contradiction, I don't mean it to be. The first two rules apply on *unimportant* occasions, and by following them you make it easier for your children to live in a society where they are in the minority. Besides the mentally gifted this includes the highly creative or talented children with lower intelligence quotients who are frequently the children with the greatest potential for outstanding accomplishment if their originality is not discouraged by conventional friends and neighbors, or in a traditional school.

Charlotte Malone, who teaches classes for parents of gifted children in San Diego and at San Fernando Valley State College, warns that parents too often object to special gifts like art or music as a "waste of time," and want their children to "get ahead" in some "practical" field.

Don't!

On the other hand, a mother of a gifted child at a panel of parents I attended recently wanted to know if she should insist on piano lessons. Don't choose an "art" for them either, but do, as she did, provide the opportunity—the piano—if you can.

It should be obvious that we can't expect average behavior from children who are not average, and it would be a shame to let them succumb to group pressure and become just like everybody else if we can start them off in early childhood with the intellectual courage to be themselves. It would be stupid—and cruel—to try to force such children into molds cut to a size that is too small for them. Yet that is what is being done by many well-meaning educators and parents all over the country. Such people think the children "will be happier," but they leave out the fact that *learning* is one of the greatest pleasures of life, and the more you are capable of learning, the happier it makes you.

The admonition not to brag is an example of a less important matter. Actually, boasting is not a common characteristic of gifted children. Terman's and other studies have shown that the gifted have an inborn humility; as Socrates believed, the truly wise know that they don't know. Bright children are less apt to be boastful than the average, since they have more reason to have confidence in themselves and don't need to bolster it up (at least in the intellectual area). They do *need* that confidence, however, if they are going to put their marvelous ideas into practice (like Benjamin

Franklin's kite, for example). So people, especially teachers, who try to "take them down a peg," are shooting down a rocket on the way to the moon.

As parents, my husband and I may have made a mistake when our fifteen-year-old son was #2 in U. S. Boys' Tennis (a sport we recommend highly for gifted children especially). One day when he was about to play another good player, we overheard David say, disgustedly, "I couldn't lose to *him*."

Since our son had always been a nice boy we wanted him to stay that way, so we lit into him. He took it to heart, and—in the next tournament he lost to that boy for the first time. The question seems to be whether you want to raise a champion athlete or a modest person; it does take a great deal of confidence to be #1 in the world at anything. It is possible of course to be a champion who has both confidence and compassion—but it's difficult.

However it was David's own choice that, after college when he was very near the top, he gave up tournament tennis to become a Ph.D., a teacher of medieval history, and an idealistic family man.

This brings up another rule; parents have no business making a choice of vocation for any child. Children often do follow in their fathers' footsteps, but all you can do is exemplify a worthwhile and satisfying career—as my husband, a college English professor, in fact did. Johnny too wanted to teach—math.

The other day I met a father, a successful Negro educator, who was very concerned about his son, who had an IQ based on the Binet test, at age ten, of almost 180. But the boy had not, he felt, fulfilled his promise. He had finished high school and gone to college, but then dropped out.

"I don't know where he is now," the father said, and I could sense his unspoken disappointment. "He's not doing anything— just traveling around."

"How old is he?" I asked.

"He's twenty."

I couldn't tell him what's going to happen to his son, but I do know that twenty is the age for boys to wander through the world. At about seventeen, the year his boy went to college, they get a sudden surge of independence from parents and other adults. This is true of all boys but especially of the gifted. They are thinking things through, discarding the outmoded conventions and unthinking maxims and hypocrisies too many of us live by. They often rebel in college, become "radicals," lose their "religion," even if they were formerly orthodox Jews or devout Catholics. But (the older you get, the more boys you see through this stage) a few years later when they've sown the traditional "wild oats" they usually become more conservative as they mature. I've seen them, boys and some girls too, return, like the Prodigal Son, or Peer Gynt, to the home, to the church, to society.

"Everyone has a mass of bad work in him which he will have to work off and get rid of before he can do better," Samuel Butler wrote in *The Way of All Flesh,* "and indeed, the more lasting a man's ultimate good work, the more sure he is to pass through a time, and perhaps a very long one, in which there seems to be very little hope for him at all. We must all sow our spiritual wild oats."

Butler himself was the son of a minister who sent him to Cambridge to prepare for the ministry. But he went to New Zealand and worked on a sheep ranch! After he came back to England he composed music, painted pictures which were exhibited in the Royal Academy, and wrote a novel about a utopian land where there is no machinery (Erewhon, which is an anagram of nowhere). Later he wrote the even more famous *Way of All Flesh.*

I told this father about Samuel Butler, and added, "You mustn't expect your son to be like everybody else. He's one in a million."

He said, "You know, my son wanted to go to Australia and work on a sheep ranch!"

I can sympathize. It must be even harder for a father whose son is exceptionally gifted in a minority which needs these gifts more than they are needed anywhere else—just to "let him be."

Which brings us to another suggestion.

This will be an answer to these questions: How do you "discipline" a gifted child? Should you refrain? How permissive should you be? It makes sense to say that the parents of a young man or

woman of twenty who has exceptional mental ability or talent—
often, though not necessarily, much greater than their own—must
expect him to make his own decisions.

But there was a time in the lives of these gifted sons and daughters when you were smarter than they were! When a child of
exactly five years has an IQ of 150, which he will probably have
within ten or fifteen points as he grows older, he is one in a
thousand children, but he has what is called a "mental age" of
seven years and four months. So you still have quite a few things
to teach this child, *and you should*. Undisciplined creativity usually
results in nothing getting done (a lazy Sir Isaac Newton could have
seen the apple fall, had an idea—and done nothing about it);
undisciplined genius may turn to evil instead of to good.

The probabilities indicate that when this same child is twelve
years old with an IQ of 150 he will have a mental age of nineteen,
which is considerably higher than the mental age of average adults.
By this time, if you—his parents—are not that gifted yourselves
you will have become increasingly aware that your child knows
more than you do, at least in the "cognitive" (knowledge) area;
but remember that a parent of average or even below average
mental ability may still have more to offer in the "affective" realm
of feeling, and of values. The same rules apply to all parents of all
children, no matter what their respective IQs: from earliest childhood on, give your children plenty of love, praise and respect, and
give them an increasing amount of responsibility and independence
each year up to a mature (but these days maturity comes early)
adulthood.

It's important for all parents, but especially for parents of the
gifted who will be leaders in our society, to exemplify and teach
a set of values, which the mentally gifted will understand even
better than the average child; and this must be done well before
the age of six. "A child's character is largely formed by the age of
six," psychologists have been telling us for years; the gifted child's
character *may* largely be formed by the age of four, since his
mental age may be six at that time.

A three-year-old of ours came to me one day with a very red

face. "Would it be all right if I took a nickel out of your pocketbook?" she asked in a scared voice.

I swallowed a chuckle (they are so cute). "Oh, *no*, honey," I said solemnly. "That would be *stealing.*"

"Well," she gulped, and her face got even redder, "I already did."

After a moment of stern deliberation, while she quaked, I told her it was good of her to tell me, and that she should go and put it back. She did, with great relief, and from that day on my purse was as safe as a safe—with her. My other children went through similar incidents; most children do. That's how they learn.

When Johnny and a little pal stole some crackerjacks at the corner grocery at the age of five or six (the friendly grocer thought I ought to know) and Johnny *wouldn't* admit it, I spanked him. (This must be what educators mean by anal authoritarianism!)

"That hurt," he said piteously.

"It was meant to," I agreed.

"Well, I'm not used to it," he told me.

But it made the necessary impression. He didn't steal, and I can't remember his telling lies anymore (honest!).

They *don't* learn, if parents don't consider honesty at an early age important.

I've always thought it one of the most important of all values, and it has to be 100 percent, which you can't expect with most virtues. Jane Addams's father, one of the better parents in *Cradles of Eminence,* told her that mental integrity comes before everything else. And when you teach your children to be honest, not only with money but with words, you are also encouraging their originality, which is essential to creativity. Too many parents discourage honest statements in favor of what's conventional, and this is like destroying a child's gifts.

This doesn't mean courtesy and kindness aren't just as important. It isn't necessary to go around hurting people's feelings; we can always keep our mouths shut.

If you love your children, you want them to be good and to be happy; the two go together at least as far as any permanent well-being is concerned. You can't just let them do anything they want to do (like taking drugs "for kicks"); they don't even *want* you to let them do anything they want to, as many child psychologists have pointed out.

"Mother, can I wear high heels?" Sheila Mary asked me in the seventh grade. (Now there's a problem you won't encounter today!)

"No," I said, expecting the usual argument.

"Good," she said.

The type of discipline is not important as long as you persist in it as long as it's needed, and do it *because you love them,* because you care what kind of a character they have. You do whatever works with that particular child at that particular moment, but you have to be continually ingenious because all children are different—I used different methods with four children in the same family. But it was always based on the golden mean—not too permissive, not too strict.

You have to keep asking yourself which are the real values, and which the false, or conventional ones. The younger generation today make a good point when they rebel at hypocrisies such as *false* modesty (prudery), false patriotism (chauvinism), or a hollow education. There are also some much less important "virtues" which the mother of a highly creative child, particularly, may have to dispense with, and the chief of these is "neatness."

Creative children need *things* to create with; the highly regarded English "Infant Schools" call these *stuff.* Heaven help the creative children of a compulsive housekeeper! They make things, they collect things, they do experiments, and they don't want you to throw them away. Even worse, they don't want you to move something they are making, like a bridge of blocks in the middle of the living room floor. I remember telling Johnny, when he was two, to put his blocks away when he got through playing.

"I don't *get* through playing," he said.

You often have to decide which is more important, the development of your child's gifts, or what the neighbors will think. This takes us back to that important Rule Three: you must not be too concerned about what other people think, and you must not teach your child to knuckle under to public opinion except in matters

Creative children are neither compulsively conforming nor non-conforming, but free to conform or nonconform depending upon what is true, beautiful, right. (Photo courtesy E. Paul Torrance, University of Georgia.)

Some educational objectives can best be assessed by group tests rather than by individual tests. (Courtesy E. Paul Torrance.)

Studying and hypothesizing the reason for changes. (Courtesy E. Paul Torrance.)

Conversations with the marionette clown motivate problem solving, story writing, drawing and painting. (Courtesy E. Paul Torrance.)

New Haven's Educational Center for the Arts is a regional program for young artists of high school age who are talented in the arts and whose needs cannot be met by most high school curricula. The center, which has as its primary purpose the continuous development of outstanding talents, serves the 13 school districts of the Greater New Haven Region. Comprehensive instruction is given in art, dance, cinematography, still photography, video tape, music and theater. (Illustration courtesy DeWitt Zuse, Director; artist, William L. Lyle.)

Three 50-minute creative dramatics sessions produced campfire skits for Hale Junior High's "gifted retreat" at School Camp Cuyamaca in the mountains east of San Diego. (Photo courtesy Mrs. Joene Bruhn and Stormy Weathers.)

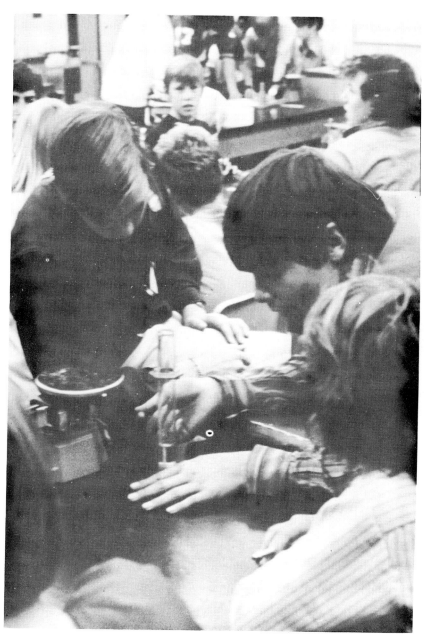

A group of sixth-grade students from Palo Alto School District meet with a group of ninth-grade Honors Science students. The ninth graders act as teachers. (Photo courtesy Ruthe A. Lundy.)

Mary Jane Cyga's advanced classes at Einstein Junior High made
picture books and educational games; they set off with them to
Knox Elementary School. (Photo courtesy San Diego City
Schools.)

Children at Knox Elementary School enjoying their books and games. (Courtesy San Diego City Schools.)

Teacher at work . . . boning up on archeology. (Courtesy San Diego City Schools.)

Mrs. Lawana Trout—Oklahoma Teacher of the Year 1964, National Teacher of the Year 1965—teaching a group of students at the inaugural program of the Gifted Students Foundation, Dallas, Summer 1971. (Courtesy Dr. Simmons.)

Fifth-Sixth—grade seminar at Jackson School studies on site at Pacific tide pools. (Photo courtesy San Diego City Schools.)

Individualization requires organization. This is how they handle modular flexible scheduling at Marshall High School, Portland, Oregon. (Photos courtesy Betty Jensen.)

Teenagers student-teaching at Temple Beth Israel's exciting school-after-school for the study of the Hebrew language, history, and religion in San Diego. A staff of 68 teenagers and 50 adult teachers challenge the traditional attitude that kids only go because "their parents will kill 'em if they don't." (Photo by William Kugel, courtesy Dr. Lawrence Meyers, Director of Education.)

At Talcott Mountain Science Center in Connecticut, staff meteorologist Eric Danielson shows students how to use an optical theodolite to track weather balloons and determine speed of winds aloft. (Courtesy Dr. William Vassar.)

Administrators of gifted programs take classes, too. (Photo courtesy San Diego City Schools.)

In the San Diego City Schools' popular Elementary Gifted Typing Program, Cindy Izuno receives an award. (Photo courtesy Dorothy Mason.)

Independent study can also be cooperative study. (Courtesy Ned Wilson, Independent Study Center, Morse High School.)

Geoff Quinn campaigns in the 1860 elections, when La Jolla High's Independent Study Center plays the simulation game "Division" in a three-week unit on events leading up to the Civil War. (Photo by Rolf Benirschke, one of the students.)

Students individualize their own study carrels . . .

and use them.

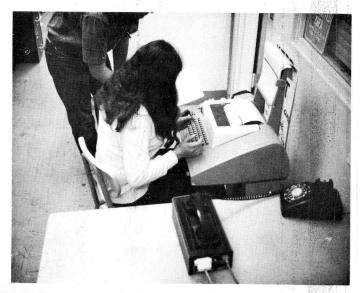

Mel Zeddies, "tutorial adviser," was determined to provide his kids with computers.

There's always something interesting to watch. (Photos in this sequence courtesy of Dr. Mel Zeddies, Samuel F. B. Morse High School, Independent Study Center.)

Since the Illinois Gifted Program is concerned with getting students involved in creative activities, and is also concerned with encouraging teachers to be more creative, the teachers who attend its workshops experience a lot of creative activities. This teacher is participating in "Uncle Wiggly's Curious and Colorful Poster Conspiracy." (Photo by Joe Wayman.)

of minor importance; in those, you should certainly teach him to be courteous and kind.

What else can parents do? Certainly parents should talk to and *listen to* their children, and try to answer their multitudinous questions; read to them before they can read, afterwards provide books and encyclopedias, get them library cards; take them to operas, plays, museums, concerts, on nature walks; teach them what you as parents have to offer, such as taking an engine apart or playing the piano; see that they have lessons in other areas that interest them BUT DON'T FILL UP ALL THEIR TIME. Gifted people of all ages have a great need of time for themselves, alone.

Where the school district provides special cluster classes in some of the elementary schools and special high school programs for the gifted, the parents may need to provide transportation to the central schools if they are not in the neighborhood. The chief problem is obvious. What about the parents who can't afford concerts and encyclopedias, who don't have a second car for the mother to transport the child to the special school? What about parents who are too busy or not interested?

Unfortunately, this is why we *must* do more for the "deprived" gifted, rich or poor, and why they are harder to identify in the first place. There are no easy solutions, but this is why federal funds for the "disadvantaged" are more plentiful now that our country has become conscious of this inequity; *every school district should take advantage of these funds.* The Report to Congress tells us that very few are doing so. Parents can speak through the PTA or their Gifted Association or Congressman or the Board of Education to get these funds, and use them.

Professors Thomas and Crescimbeni, authorities we have quoted in the controversies at the beginning of each chapter, say that a vocal parent group demanding the Board of Education do more for the gifted children in the community *cannot be ignored.* Unfortunately, school principals find it very hard to ignore the parents who call up and complain about new programs they *don't* like. So if your child is in a special program you like, let the principal know.

It would be a kindness if parents who are providing transportation for a child of their own to a special gifted program would also pick up one or two children who couldn't otherwise go. This would help not only the child who is deprived of cultural and/or material advantage but also their own children who are often deprived of chances to be thoughtful of the needs of others. Studies have shown that the "élite" are *more* naturally compassionate, more conscious of social injustices, than the average person, but too many "rich kids" seldom have a chance to develop this valuable trait. We don't realize how selfishness, or at least self-centeredness, can dominate the lives of the well-to-do. The experience of "busing" a gifted friend from another community to a special school would be more worthwhile than ballet lessons or a season ticket to the opera; perhaps it would also be possible to take the friend along to the opera.

Most parents are delighted when their children are selected for special programs, or when acceleration is suggested by the school, but many others are not. The average-ability parent of a good student may worry, because he doesn't trust anything new; it's the gifted who are, by and large, the innovators.

Should parents accept the recommendation of the school for his child's education? Most educators will give you an unequivocal "yes." But too often the parent finds himself in the dilemma I faced when I had to decide between two doctors: most educators will agree that you should do as they recommend, but then they recommend different things! So at least *sometimes* the parent—who knows the child better than anyone else—should refuse to accept the school's opinions.

My husband and I battled our children's way through grade school by insisting on an occasional skipped grade when we knew they already knew everything in that grade; no other plan was offered for gifted children in our small town. We had both skipped grades in our childhoods with good results, and we are in a position to say, now that our children are through school, that it also worked out well for them. Frea graduated #1 in her high school class, completed college *magna cum laude,* and is now happily married, has five children, and runs a Peace Corps Trainee program every summer. Sheila Mary—her own idea—went from her junior year in high school to college when that opportunity was first extended.

"But you'll miss your senior year in high school!" I protested. That was the year I had the most fun, what with being in love and all the extracurricular activities.

"I'll have fun in college," she said, and she did. Now, she is married, with four children, and works mornings as a teachers' aide, while they're in school.

As for Johnny, who was a senior in high school when he died, moving ahead seemed to give him two extra years of living "to his fullest capacity." And he had lived four years longer than the doctors thought he possibly could.

David, the one who went through all the grades, was the one who said, when he got his Ph.D., "I've hated school ever since I was six."

On the other hand, if you want to hear of cases of people who wish they hadn't skipped, you'll find letters in Louise Bates Ames's *Is Your Child in the Wrong Grade?*

I don't pretend to be an authority on what someone else should do, but I do believe parents have rights regarding the education of their children which are often high-handedly ignored. Dr. William Vassar of Connecticut, one of the most dedicated and influential people in gifted education, said in a talk in San Diego the other day that parents do have "the right of refusal." Mrs. Ames, who believes in grouping children by ability but not in acceleration, says parents have the right to insist that their children remain in a grade if they are not ready for the next grade, but not the right to ask that they be put in a higher grade.

How then can parents decide when to follow the school's recommendation for a gifted child and when not to? If the school wants to do something special for your child because they have given him tests and observed his school behavior and decided to spend state or federal funds designated for the gifted on him (or her), then I think by all means you should cooperate in every way you can, even if it's something new you don't know as much about as they do. While some special programs have faults which are ironed out during experimentation, I have been visiting innovative schools and pilot programs for three years now, and I have yet to see one that wasn't better (for gifted or any other children) than the egg-crate classrooms I went to and my children went to; and my husband agrees.

And you can always ask the kids!

It is when a school wants to hold a child back, to ignore his gifts, to keep him from learning, that you must try to do something for him yourself, provided of course that you are sure he is gifted, and that you are not merely ambitious for him. Such parents do exist, and they are a pain in the neck to their own children as well as to the schools. But many parents are called ambitious when in fact they are simply standing up for their children's right to the freedom to learn.

If a school system refuses to do anything at all for gifted children, and also has a blanket rule that NO child shall EVER be allowed to skip a grade, and you can't budge them in this decision, then I suggest that you move!

One last point (for emphasis): But be careful not to make a gifted child your Life Work—it's *his* life! Or hers . . .

                                        Sincerely,
                                        Owenita Sanderlin

8
Should Pupils Be Grouped by Ability?

MONTAIGNE (16th century): *Such as according to our common way of thinking undertake, with one and the same lesson, and the same measure of direction, to instruct several boys of differing and unique capacities, are infinitely mistaken; and 'tis no wonder, if in a whole multitude of scholars, there are not found above two or three who bring away any good account of their time and discipline.*

JAMES BRYANT CONANT (scientist, educator, former Harvard President, 1959): *Students should be grouped by ability, subject by subject.*

(in 1967 follow-up study): *At the time my first study was made . . . "ability grouping" was a highly controversial subject. As I then recorded, I have met competent teachers who argued vigorously for the heterogeneous grouping in all classes. . . . Other teachers were equally certain that justice cannot be done to either the bright student or the slow reader if both receive instruction in the same class. The controversy seems to have subsided . . . for 96.5 per cent of the principals [in 2000 high schools] responded affirmatively to the following question: Do you group students by ability in one or more academic subjects?*

LOUISE BATES AMES (1967): *Children of superior endowment should certainly be grouped with others of similar endowment in a top group.*

JOHN HOLT (1969): *I am altogether opposed to any kind of ability grouping in school.*

101

WILLIAM GLASSER (educator, writer, M.D., 1969): *Tracking, or homogeneous grouping by ability is bad not only because of its effect on the students; it also has an insidious and destructive effect upon teachers.*

NEIL POSTMAN AND CHARLES WEINGARTNER (teachers and writers, 1969): *. . . there is hardly a school in the country that has not organized children into groups labeled "dumb" so that both their teachers and they can know exactly what they "are."*

MARK R. LOHMAN (a UC-Riverside professor testifying before a Senate Committee on Equal Educational Opportunity, as reported in *Los Angeles Times,* November 14, 1971): *Schools grouping pupils by ability tests are signalling to the lower level students a clear, devastating social message which will change his life. "Those guys are better than I am. I'm not going anywhere," a student will think, then give up and accept his fate.*

SIDNEY P. MARLAND, JR. (U.S. Commissioner of Education, in a report to Congress, 1971): *Clear support for special groupings was found in New York, in the Major Work Classes in Cleveland, in Los Angeles, and in numerous other locales. Participants showed improvement not only in academic areas but also in personal and social areas.*

GERALD STANLEY (Coordinator, Secondary Gifted Program, Garden Grove, California, in a talk in San Diego, February 23, 1972): *All this talk about undemocratic methods of grouping kids is hogwash. Unless there's some effort at grouping there's no gifted program.*

JOHN I. GOODLAD (noted for his work on nongraded schools, 1965): *Fifth graders commonly read . . . at levels ranging all the way from the second or third grade to the ninth or tenth. . . . [The child] can be in the fifth grade for arithmetic computation, the . . . seventh for spelling . . . the eighth for word meaning . . .*

and the tenth for language and yet be officially registered in the sixth grade. . . . However uneven his attainments, there is a group within the open room working on his level in each subject, and a teacher to go with it. If he learns rapidly, he can move from week to week to a group at a more advanced level of achievement.

GEORGE I. THOMAS AND JOSEPH CRESCIMBENI (1966): *Every pupil in the heterogeneous class can benefit from the stimulation applied by a few extremely bright pupils. Much has been said about the waste of intellect when gifted students are left in heterogeneous classrooms. But . . . these pupils have a great deal to gain from working in an atmosphere where they can excel and be acknowledged as leaders.*

JOHN CURTIS GOWAN AND E. PAUL TORRANCE (1971): *. . . it is what happens in class, and not how it is grouped, that counts.*

WILLIAM VASSAR (Consultant for the Gifted, Connecticut State Department of Education, speaking in San Diego, 1972): *I really don't feel that gifted child education can be handled in the regular classroom.*

It's interesting to note from this controversy that while the majority of conservative opinion has turned more and more toward ability grouping, which it was formerly against, many radical or anyhow innovative thinkers are now turning away from it.

Jean Piaget, the Swiss psychologist, who carries weight with education people in both the old camp and the new, says that *everyone has constantly urged that schooling should be adapted to the child.*

It should be hard to find anyone who would not agree with this statement—in theory; yet in practice the majority of schools are still working against it. We still support education *en masse:* teach children of the same age the same things in the same room even if we have to organize the kids into "ability groups" to accomplish this purpose—only we never do accomplish it.

Reading is the best example of the failure of this time-honored system of grouping: it goes way back to the robins, the blue jays and the orioles. But many gifted children learn to read before they get to school, some as early as two years old, and this formerly frowned-upon practice is now being encouraged—by *some* authorities. I hope the new young first-grade teachers are happier about it than they used to be!

Other bright children do *not* learn to read even when they get to school because they are bored by the content of their books or the structured methods of teaching reading—at the rate of about one sentence per child per day, in "recitation." Gifted teachers have always managed to get around this by creative methods, but with large classes and no teachers' aides they find it hard to find time enough to tutor the children who most need help in learning how to read, and at the same time to keep the fast learners interested.

It has been said that as many as fifty percent of all children get to high school without the reading skills needed to tackle their high school subjects. This should be all the indication we need that the traditional reading methods don't work. When teachers (in the old-fashioned-type schools which still predominate) divide their classes into birds, flowers, A and B groups or whatever "secret" code they use, not a kid in the room is so "dumb" that he doesn't know he's in the slow, bottom, or inferior group, and that the other kids are better readers than he is.

This is why I could never see why parents and teachers continue to insist that it's more "democratic" (or kinder) to keep "A" kids in classes with "F" kids *of the same age*. It seems to me that is undemocratic, and bad for the slower learner's self-confidence (the Self-Image, in Pedagoguese). Robert Rosenthal and Lenore Jacobson conducted an experiment with a different type of grouping which they reported on in *Pygmalion in the Classroom*. They told teachers that some of their children had the potential to develop more rapidly than others, even though this was not a fact.

The children were not told, just the teachers, but what happened was that the pupils with "potential" did in fact develop faster than the others simply because the teachers expected them to, and treated them as if they could. They gained an average of 24.4 IQ points in one year while the control group gained only 12.

Ability grouping in age-grouped classrooms also wastes a great deal of time in duplicated effort; a second-grade fast group, for just one example, may be reading at the same level as a fourth-grade middle group. And pupils who don't know how to read at all are commonly given the same amount of time as children who could go off in a corner and read all by themselves if only they didn't have to sit in a circle and "recite" at a snail's pace (in the name of egalitarianism!).

I've never forgotten my first grade teacher, not even her name. Miss Applewhite made first grade a joy. I suppose she taught us all together to begin with—I don't remember when I learned how to read—but the minute we knew how (and it is a skill that "happens" to you suddenly, sometimes), we got to go off and "just read" one book after another, putting a bookmark in the page where we left off each day; I remember the first story I ever read was "The Little Red Hen," and that I read 26 books in first grade. It doesn't seem possible we could have *regressed* in an area of education as important as reading, does it? And yet—fifty percent? And how many of our dropouts are frustrated nonreaders, I wonder?

Ability grouping as a phrase seems to be used to mean different things, which may be one reason different educators and community members don't agree as to whether it's a good thing or not. Another word sometimes used as a synonym is *tracking*. According to the principal of a junior high school I visited recently, he could do nothing for the gifted in his school because the community was against any form of tracking or ability grouping; he simply could not set up any special class. A group of new seventh-graders who had been identified as gifted and belonged to a "cluster" in elementary school were disappointed that there was nothing like this in junior high; it had been a successful experience, filling them with enthusiasm for learning—freely, and at their own speed.

This is a common problem with gifted programs: as children move from school to school, whether from elementary to junior high or to another part of the country, they may lose benefits they've come to enjoy. This is why we must fight for the *cause* of these special children who will be so valuable (or dangerous!) to our society in the future, and we must do this in every state of the Union. The Report to Congress says we are making very little effort in all but a few states.

"California is one of the four states selected in the Report to Congress for its model gifted programs," I said to Beth Smith, president of the San Diego parents' association, "and Professor Gowan, after making an evaluation, said in his speech today that San Diego has the best program in the state."

She said, "You know, that filled me with dismay, when I know how little *we've* done yet!"

Conservative community members who believe in states rights and local control of education should scrutinize their own interests more closely, and ask themselves, "Do we want the gifted children in our community to be able to compete with the gifted in other states?"

We do have to have outstanding adults, don't we? Then why must we try so hard to hide, even to destroy, those same gifts in our children?

That slower learners need the enthusiasm of good students in their classes is one of the best arguments there is for heterogeneous classes; another is that bright children may suffer if they are put into a homogeneous group where there are "all Chiefs and no Indians," where the less aggressive may become followers rather than the leaders they would have been in a regular class.

When Johnny was in the fifth grade we lived in a suburban district where there happened to be many bright children, and as a "capable but shy" student (an earlier teacher-comment) he was a follower: he contributed to, but didn't edit, the school paper, and played left field on the baseball team. The next year when we moved to a rural area he was editor of the paper and captain of the baseball team. We felt *both* experiences were good ones; perhaps he wouldn't have done so well at School Two if he hadn't been associated with the enthusiastic children in School One. And he was happy in both schools.

Another difficulty for students in accelerated or honors classes is that it's harder to make top grades, which in high school are all-important for getting into college, and winning scholarships. The answer to this is to abolish grades, especially in gifted classes as they are set up now, and eventually in all classes. Some school systems give automatic As in gifted programs with the provision that students who don't measure up will not be retained in the program. That may be a necessity as long as grades are mandatory.

The controversy over ability grouping remains unsettled. As a debate coach in competitive tournaments I learned that given a good question, either the affirmative or the negative can *win;* also I learned that of five highly competent judges in a debate final, three can decide for one team and two for the other. Finally I learned that judges are sometimes prejudiced, and that one prejudiced judge could therefore decide who wins!

So let's admit that there are good arguments both for and against ability grouping. As Dr. Conant said, conservative opinion against it in 1958 had swung around to it in 1967. And in February 1972, at a conference attended by leaders in gifted education from all over the country, William Vassar of Connecticut said sensibly, "Ability grouping is neither good nor bad; it depends on the program." He feels that a policy of semi-separation is good, with the gifted spending some time in general classes and some in special classes.

When conservative opinion finally arrives, the pioneer thinkers have gone on ahead. This, I believe, is the case today. When John Holt says he is altogether opposed to ability grouping of any kind, we need to have read his books to know that he is also against the kind of school in which ability grouping probably is still needed. John Holt is an outstanding teacher who can teach children in heterogeneous groups, but he doesn't do it "the way it's always been done."

But Bill Vassar says, "We're at least a decade away from the public schools' meeting the needs of all the students," so we need to do something for the gifted *now*.

Special groups or classes or schools for the gifted *may* not be needed if we can re-form our elementary and secondary schools into places where every child can learn at his own speed; if we can find or retrain enough teachers who can teach in new and better ways—many of *which have already been devised;* and finally, if we can give such teachers the help they need from assistants and teachers' aides, and principals and superintendents who will support their ideas, even give them more ideas, instead of firing them for "not maintaining discipline" or for using unconventional materials instead of dull textbooks.

It won't hurt to list some of the good new ideas which may render "ability grouping," with its faults as well as its virtues, unnecessary.

Above all, there is individualization of instruction. In *Creative Teaching,* I wrote a case study of an elementary school, Silver Gate in San Diego, which was running a successful pilot project funded by the school district. The principle behind this technique, which is becoming more and more widely used throughout the country, is the same as that of the one-room "little red schoolhouse" of earlier American days (and a few exist today), where the pupils ranged in both age and ability from primary to college prep, and one teacher had to teach them all. Obviously, she had to give each child whatever he needed, whether it was how to read, or how to do algebra or Latin to get into college. She took them, as the current phrase puts it, from "where they were at" to where they wanted to go.

But because we were able, in compulsory public schools, to gather together enough children of the same age to fill at least one room, we decided one teacher could teach them all in unison, so we lectured, drilled, reviewed and tested them into a state of boredom which afflicted both slow and fast learners, because hardly a child in the room was learning what *he* wanted or needed to know or could even understand at that particular moment of mental awareness.

Many new mechanical aids for individualized instruction have been and are being devised, such as "talking typewriters," teaching machines, computer consoles, programmed textbooks, tapes, earphones and other audio-visual aids, language labs and educational television; but even more important are the new teaching techniques: the use of teachers' aides, team teaching, independent study including contract learning or individually prescribed instruction, pupil-tutors, and various combinations of these.

Almost indispensable to individualization of instruction are teachers' aides and assistants, including part-time parents, college students and community volunteers, especially those who have special skills to offer, such as teaching fourth year math where there is no teacher who can do it, or Russian or violin or Black Studies or creative writing. Such special teachers (who may or may not be paid) are called paraprofessionals, and they act as librarians, tutor small groups and so on. Parent assistants are also employed to do clerical work.

For detailed information on how to use such help, see Betty Atwell Wright's *Teacher Aides to the Rescue,* New York, John Day, 1969; Frank Riessman's *Up From Poverty,* New York, Harper & Row, 1968, which includes a description of T.A.P., the excellent program in the Washington, D.C. Model Schools; or *Teacher Assistants,* by Mel H. Robb, Columbus, Ohio, Charles E. Merrill Pub. Co., 1969.

"Team teaching" is a phrase coined in 1957 when this innovation, now widely accepted, was initiated in a Lexington, Massachusetts, high school. Simply, it is the use of a master teacher or two, with one or more assistants, to share a class or classes. The concept lends itself to many variations, such as the more complex "pontoon" system, or the Independent Studies "school within a school" with two teachers, one a math and science teacher and the other specializing in the humanities, sharing a group of gifted students for a large part of the school day. This is the plan which, after trial in one high school, is now being used successfully in the five San Diego high schools discussed in Chapter 5.

Computer-assisted instruction is another way of individualizing the basic school work to fit each pupil; so far it's limited in use for financial and organizational reasons, and because, while there are computers that can "teach" (the hardware), we don't yet have enough good teaching materials (the software) to stock the computers. "Garbage in and garbage out" is the most memorable criticism I've heard!

However, given a "talking typewriter" or a console connecting a distant elementary school to a Stanford University or other central computer, we *can* teach a child the basics of a subject like arithmetic or a language, individually at his own pace. The work of Patrick Suppes has been outstanding in this field, and it seems likely that further progress will be made. We can hope that computers will give teachers more time to do the things for kids that machines can't do.

Ideally, with computers or similar "programmed learning" in books, gifted children could gobble up the basics in any subject and forge ahead as far as their minds could take them; it could save them much valuable *time*. For slow learners, the main value is that they can take as long as they need to learn thoroughly, to understand before they go on; it also means there would be no need for comparative *grades* on "report cards." Both gifted and average or retarded learners could get "all A's" as far as they had the ability to go; the only difference would be in the time it takes.

In any kind of individualized or individually prescribed instruction or contract learning, there are no "ability groups." It's every child for himself. It is generally conceded that anyone can learn more if he has a teacher all to himself—a tutor; individualized teaching in heterogeneous, *nongraded* schools would be the nearest we could come to a tutorial system, and still maintain the added advantage of the beneficial social experiences our public schools have unquestionably provided for our children.

So it isn't a question of whether ability grouping is good or bad. The way most schools are still set up, it's probably a necessary evil, but we don't have to settle for any kind of evil; there are too many sensible solutions to the problem of how, in a school system that serves all our children, we can best serve each one of them.

There's no excuse for not making use of these new and widely tested ideas except apathy and inertia, or unthinking emotionalism —in a word, prejudice. But perhaps it is "early days" yet; perhaps we should continue to try out these techniques with the children who are *most* likely to benefit from them, and to show how they can work for others: our gifted "pioneers."

One of the bonuses in an evaluation of the outstanding gifted programs the state of Illinois is working on is precisely this "spill-over" effect. "Many of the materials and techniques introduced in gifted programs," they note, "have been utilized in other classes as well." (For information write Robert Hardy, Jr., Director Illinois Gifted Program, 1020 So. Spring, Springfield, Illinois 62706.)

Ability grouping, they feel, may be one of the most serious disadvantages of gifted programs, in that it leads to élitism: "yet there is little doubt that grouping by ability provides a unique opportunity for an intellectually stimulating class." Like William Vassar of Connecticut, they conclude that there is need of *some* ability grouping and, as I have recommended, "ultimately, the aim would be to provide individualized instruction."

9

Acceleration—or Enrichment?

MRS. NORMAL: *Your child was pushed ahead!*

MRS. BRIGHT: *It seems to me the child who gets promoted when he hasn't learned to read yet is the one who is pushed ahead.*

SIDNEY P. MARLAND, JR. (1971): *50 percent of public school educators opposed acceleration, despite research evidence that acceleration is beneficial at every level from kindergarten to college.*

JEROME BRUNER (1960): *Ideally, schools should allow students to go ahead in different subjects as rapidly as they can. But the administrative problems that are raised when one makes such an arrangement possible are almost inevitably beyond the resources that schools have available for dealing with them. The answer will probably lie in some modification or abolition of the system of grade levels in some subjects, notably mathematics, along with a program of course enrichment in other subjects.*

LEWIS TERMAN AND MELITA ODEN (1947): *It is our opinion that children of 135 IQ or higher should be promoted sufficiently to permit college entrance by the age of seventeen at the latest, and . . . a majority . . . at sixteen. Acceleration to this extent is especially desirable for those who plan to complete two or more years of graduate study in preparation for a professional career.*

Counselor of 250 gifted high school students (1972): *I think they should stay in high school till they're eighteen.*

112

LOUISE BATES AMES (1967): *Enrichment rather than pushing ahead is our recommendation for most highly superior children.*

LEWIS TERMAN AND MELITA ODEN (1947): *Unfortunately, the so-called enrichment often amounts to little more than a quantitative increase of work on the usual level.*

WILLIAM VASSAR (in a speech in San Diego, 1972): *Too many kids are getting nothing more than more of the same.*

GEORGE I. THOMAS AND JOSEPH CRESCIMBENI (1966): *Research studies have indicated that skipping grades is not harmful to gifted pupils; however, they tend to emphasize acceleration through traditional schools and not modern schools where children can take part in a broad and enriching series of activities when they have completed the basic minimum requirements. . . . If the objective is to get these pupils into college at sixteen or seventeen, the same results can be achieved by accelerating the curriculum rather than the pupil.*

JOHN I. GOODLAD (in "The Schools vs. Education," *Saturday Review,* April 19, 1969): *No need . . . to confine teaching to the hours between 9 in the morning and 3 in the afternoon, nor to delay certain subjects until high school or college.*

RUTH STRANG (1960): *A good plan seems to be to complete the first three grades in two years and the three junior high grades in two years. Some children who develop rapidly in high school may profit by advanced placement programs which enable them to save one year of college.*

ALVIN C. EURICH (1969): *. . . early admission to college . . . began in 1951 in twelve colleges and has now been extended to many more on the basis of satisfactory results. . . . admission with advanced standing [having taken some college courses while in high* *school*] . . . *too, has proved effective.* . . . *Both of these methods tend to reduce boredom and wasteful human activity.*

CHARLES SILBERMAN (1970): . . . *in the elementary grades, an able student can be absent from school for an entire week and, quite literally, catch up with all he has missed in a single morning.*

R. W. GERARD (Dean of Graduate Studies, University of California at Irvine, 1967): *With the use of computers the kindergarten through twelfth grade years could be reduced by as much as 3 years without leaving out anything of worth.* [This was not limited to the gifted.]

GEORGE I. THOMAS AND JOSEPH CRESCIMBENI (1966): . . . *many teachers and . . . administrators are opposed to acceleration programs as a matter of principle. They will argue that the accelerated students will not be mature enough, but beyond this generalization they tend to get lost in vague generalities that have been refuted time and time again.*

JOHN CURTIS GOWAN AND GEORGE DEMOS (1964): *Somewhere between 1930 and 1933, coincident with the depression and extending on until the end of World War II, there . . . was a de-emphasis on matters . . . related to gifted children. Acceleration was damned and grouping ostracized.* . . . *[many] of our present educators, who were in training at the time, received their indoctrination against special education for the able.*

WILLIAM VASSAR (speaking, 1972): *There is the problem of the resistance of teachers to students who can attend class twice a week and do all the work.*

ROBERT F. DEHAAN (psychology professor and specialist in the study of acceleration, 1963): *When students become excited about education (as they usually do in accelerated learning programs), when they begin to see the importance of learning, when a school*

*emphasizes achievement and develops a tradition of excellence, a
new dimension is added to school life . . . respect for the realm of
the intellect. . . . Average pupils often wish to participate in the
interesting experiences their faster classmates are enjoying. . . .
Teachers can hold out modified accelerated learning programs as
incentives to average students.*

High school sophomore in a gifted program (overheard, 1972):
*My educational objectives? I want to learn everything about every-
thing!*

JEAN PIAGET (1969): *Those individuals who are most gifted, and
of most possible use to society may waste months or years of their
life at precisely that age when the new ideas that will shape their
future careers are taking place within them.*

Perhaps acceleration is the wrong word.

For too long we have been *decelerating*—slowing down—millions of children who could have learned much more than they did
learn, and in a much shorter time. We have spent billions of
property-tax dollars to keep elementary and secondary boys and
girls who were ready to go on to college in our schools for from
one to three years longer than they needed to be there, and either
bored them or conventionalized their creative minds so that when
they got to college their original endowment of intellectual curiosity
was "turned off," perhaps for good.

We have ignored the fact that a great many children have, in
fact, gone through our schools in less than thirteen years, and
become successful and well-adjusted adults; we were too busy
publicizing the convenient myths about immaturity, maladjustment
and emotional instability.

Certainly there are cases of men and women who skipped grades
in childhood (the only form of acceleration there was then) who
blame later psychological troubles or difficulties in school on the

skipped grade. Louise Bates Ames, in *Is Your Child in the Wrong Grade?* cites some of them, but she doesn't print *any* letters from people like me or my husband or his sister or some of our best friends or our children (now grown) or their friends for whom skipping a grade or two has turned out to be of benefit. That wouldn't have supported her thesis, which is that children are sometimes not ready to do first grade work at age six, but that even the brightest six-year-olds will find plenty to challenge them in grade one and in the ensuing grades. This opinion is shared by the majority of the American public, and Mrs. Ames and the Gesell Institute of Child Development are outstanding authorities who have done much for parents and children; I venture to disagree, as do many other authorities, only in this area.

"Yes, your child is *capable* of doing the work of a higher grade," a principal of the traditional school will admit, "but in our experience children who skip grades are bound to have emotional problems later on."

True. *Don't we all?*

We don't publicize stories of gifted children who *didn't* skip grades and are emotionally maladjusted by the time they get to college; nor do we mention children of average ability who didn't skip grades, yet had emotional problems in later life.

As long as objections to acceleration are based on emotional prejudices such as fear, jealousy or anti-intellectualism in parents, teachers or administrators, selected cases of sixteen-year-olds who have nervous breakdowns in college can always be found to "prove" the point. My own personal citations of selected cases to make my point are just as unscientific.

So we have to turn to the many unbiased studies which have been made in this area—and widely ignored—for at least forty years. If you want ammunition, or need to be convinced, some examples of studies which concluded that acceleration does not harm children are:

Noel Keys, "Adjustment of Under Age Students in High School," *Psychological Bulletin* 32, October, 1935.

Thelburn L. Engle, "A Study of the Effects of School Accelera-
tion Upon the Personality and School Adjustment of High
School and University Students," *Journal of Educational
Psychology* 29 (October, 1938).

Joseph Justman, "Personal and Social Adjustments of Intellectually Gifted Accelerants and Non-accelerants in Junior High
School," *School Review,* 61 (November, 1953) also one on
their academic achievements in the same magazine 62 (March,
1954).

Norman Mirman, "Are Accelerated Students Socially Maladjusted?" *Elementary School Journal* 62, (February 1962).

In the past ten years, although it sometimes doesn't seem so, we
have come a long way toward a more reasonable kind of education. At least we now *have* some better ways of teaching children,
even though these ideas have not yet been put into widespread
practice. We have some new answers to the old problems, such as
Professor Gowan's searching question, "How do we harmonize the
opposing principles of developing each individual to his maximum
and at the same time provide for the greatest general good through
a common education?"—which he calls a "peculiarly American
problem."

When my husband and I were children (*before* 1930), the only
thing the schools could do for a child who knew the material in his
grade was to skip him, and they did. I can't remember that anyone
ever got uptight about it.

When I was in 2-A (we had half-grades then), Ralph Waldo
Emerson School was having a crowded classroom problem, possibly
because of a baby boom from World War I. One day a portly
silver-haired teacher from 2-B walked in and said, "How many of
you can read?"

Quite a few of us stood up; Miss Applewhite's free-reading
method had worked well.

"Come with me," said Miss Noble, and we were in 2-B.

My husband had similar experiences, which resulted in his
getting his Ph.D. at the age of 23, just in time: our first baby was
born nine months later, during his first year of teaching. The year
before that we lived on $900.

But now, two generations later, with our children's children in school, there are alternatives to skipping grades or getting "enrichment," which in our children's schools was nothing but more arithmetic problems or other "busy work" at the same level of learning; outstanding among these is John Goodlad's "nongraded" school. Unfortunately, in too many school districts in the United States, these alternatives are still being ignored, and in such cases skipping is still the only thing that can be done for a gifted child. I strongly advocate it for any well-adjusted, mature, physically able child who is obviously not learning anything new in the grade he is in. This is what I recommend whether a doubtful parent wonders whether to accept the school's recommendation for acceleration or whether a determined parent has to fight for it.

How lucky you are if you live in an advanced school district which is at least trying out the new ideas, including a new meaning for the word "enrichment," as well as individualized and/or non-graded schools, or plans for independent study which "accelerate the curriculum" rather than the child.

Some of the best gifted programs in the country have for a number of years been based on genuine enrichment activities and materials which "broaden and deepen" the child's knowledge; they provide *different* things to learn, not just more of the same. This is what an educator means when he tells you a special program, in order to receive funding from the state or federal government, must be "not quantitatively but qualitatively different."

All the innovations mentioned in the last chapter as improvements over ability grouping (in its old sense) are equally applicable when it comes to acceleration. For convenience I'll put them in a list, although of course some of them overlap or are used in combinations. I will also add others.

Individualization of instruction.
Team or pontoon teaching.
Teaching assistants or aides as tutors, librarians, etc.
Paraprofessional teachers for special subjects.
Computer-assisted instruction, educational TV and other technological innovations.

Nongraded or ungraded schools, or combinations of grades.

Enrichment through field trips and other community resources, travelling libraries, access to laboratories and many other *genuinely* enriching activities.

Flexible scheduling.

Planned acceleration in special programs for the gifted.

Independent study (various plans).

Early admission to college.

Advanced placement, or admission to college with advanced standing, having taken college courses while in high school or by tests.

Summer school, not just for extras but to meet requirements.

Year-round school plans, with enrichment in time-off periods.

Multi-class or cross-grade groupings.

Honors and advanced classes and seminars.

Contract learning or individually prescribed instruction (IPI).

The Unit approach (building the individual curriculum around a report or study in a major-interest area).

Released-time programs (student may leave school for other cultural, educational or career-job opportunities for part of the day).

Community or other educational programs after school or on Saturdays.

Work programs (the student spends half the day or other periods of time in a career-oriented job or apprenticeship).

Simulation games (See *The Guide to Simulation Games For Education and Training,* Information Resources, Inc., 1675 Mass. Ave., Cambridge, Mass. 02138)

Self-teaching courses, including correspondence courses sometimes paid for by the school.

Programmed learning (a business school cut an accounting course from 19 to about 2 hours by programmed instruction).

Qualifying examinations for course credit; "challenge" tests.

Early entrance to school for children who can read.

Special schools for gifted or talented children.

California Project Talent (see *Final Report,* California State Department of Education, 1969) describes a successful acceleration demonstration in elementary school, based on similar programs previously tried elsewhere in the country and considered "efficient and effective." Instead of skipping a grade, with the concomitant "missed" areas of learning, second graders went to a special summer session to learn the material of the third grade, and in the fall entered fourth grade. Only 9 of the 522 accelerated children had any serious trouble in the advanced grade, and in all 9 cases their inclusion had been considered doubtful to begin with.

Interestingly, the chief "unsolved difficult problem" the study came up with was "unfavorable attitudes toward acceleration" from teachers and parents who went to school in the 1920–1940 period, and administrators were not willing to tolerate their "incessant criticism."

Yet today more and more educators who have studied the problem are recommending one or two years of acceleration for gifted students which, as I have said before, would save us taxpayers a lot of money!

The list of possible ways to accelerate studies increases every year, since one new concept opens up others; for example, the now widely-accepted team teaching plan, which broke into the sacred one-teacher-dominated "egg-crate" classroom in 1957, has branched out into a variety of plans. The most exciting one I've visited is the one I've mentioned before, the "school within a school" for a group of gifted students who spend part or all of the high school day in independent study under the leadership of two teachers, specialists in their fields of math-science and the humanities.

This idea in itself is likely to work out in various ways with different student-needs and teacher-qualifications or personalities or "teaching styles." It may take place during or after class hours. For example, the Enfield, Connecticut, student-run social studies laboratory with Frank Gross as "faculty friend" started in 1967. A $1000 state grant equipped the lab, and students use it enthusiastically in study periods and after school.

In San Diego and elsewhere in the country some of the junior high schools, under the enthusiastic leadership of special counselors for the gifted, have started "I. S." programs too.

The nucleus for these independent study programs may be a special room which "belongs" to the group, like the one at Morse

High School, described in Chapter 5. Parents sometimes provide carpeting or the kids piece it together with squares of different-colored rug samples. They have "water-rings" to sit in, or sometimes perch on file cabinets to have class discussions; some use chairs! There are bookshelves, with books and magazines contributed by their dedicated teachers or the community; Cecil Munsey, a full-time District Resource Teacher for secondary schools, and Ole Kittleson for the elementary schools, collect such contributions, suggest programs and speakers, help out in their own areas of special skill (Mr. Munsey is a writer, Mr. Kittleson an actor), write up the programs and do a thousand and one other "resourceful" things to build these valuable gifted programs.

These colorful independent study centers become an incentive—as Robert DeHaan pointed out in the introductory debate—to other students in the school, by making learning look much more interesting. At Morse High School, I noticed several admiring visitors hanging around, and they seemed to be welcome. One of them said she hoped she could "make it" next year.

"Half the school wants to be in it," the kids told me.

The teacher-counselor helps the students plan their own curriculums, and these plans vary widely. So far, in the junior high area especially, all that can be conceded by the powers-that-be is a slightly modified program of regular classes; but advanced or honors classes are usually available, and in fact are prescribed if the school is to receive state funds for the identified gifted students. And the counselors may arrange for them to have one or two free periods to spend in the library, in their study-room, on a special field trip or in other "enriching" ways, such as the Sunshine School program at Hale Junior High, instead of just going to Study Hall.

Another of the more common but limited plans is to have two "back-to-back" periods for English and social studies with a master-teacher who can also get his students released from other classes, when they can take care of the work and there are worthwhile activities their special teacher can supervise, such as the trip to the tidepools, a court trial, Student Congress or speech tournament. Exceptional ability as a teacher is needed in this plan.

Another plan used in O'Farrell Junior High under imaginative Dan Shannon is to meet the gifted students in a home-room, and let them take as many different classes as they can handle by showing up only two or three times a week in each one, but keeping up with the class work; in fact, these kids do extra reports besides. As William Vassar says, you have to overcome the resistance of teachers to this idea.

At the "left" end of the spectrum is the self-contained group of gifted students for whom "no bells toll." Much of their work is self-initiated; they may build units around their special interests, and the master teacher can guide them in directions that will encompass most of the skills they would ordinarily get in a regular English, history, science or math class. This means the master teachers are also counselors.

High school students like these are sometimes released to take college classes on local campuses, or as elementary pupils they may visit junior high schools. Obviously this is going to lead to acceleration—or could we call it *exhilaration?* They learn because they want to learn, because they are free to learn.

Such programs are so new that not much has been written about "independent study" except in a very general way. A good chapter on the subject is to be found in *The Junior High and Middle Schools,* by Alvin W. Howard and George C. Stoumbis. Among the schools these authors discuss briefly are ungraded Melbourne High School in Florida (for qualifying students); a New York school, grades 7–12 (any interested student may apply); a Pennsylvania school with grades 9, 10 in which 97 percent of the student body was involved (see "Independent Study—For *All* Students" in *Phi Delta Kappan,* 47 [March 1966] Allan J. Glatthorn and J. F. Ferderbar); Winnetka, Illinois, Junior High School; and Theodore, Alabama, High School, grades 7–12.

One of the most exciting things about gifted education right now is the way the different states are sending representatives to observe each other's programs; in one month, in San Diego, I met consultants who had flown in from St. Louis, Missouri, Illinois and Connecticut as well as from other parts of California; and a combined convention of CAG, NAG and TAG was held in Long Beach in February 1972. These playful nicknames stand for California Association for Gifted Children, the National Association for Gifted Children, and The Association for Gifted, a division of the national Council for Exceptional Children.

Programs for the gifted are bound to differ, to evolve from the needs of individual students and probably to change from year to year. The outstanding Illinois Plan is based on this premise: "participating school districts are urged to develop programs that are as innovative and diverse as the talents of their students." The state provides consultants, materials, inservice training and funds; in order to qualify for these, the individual school presents its plan of individualization, independent study or curricular modification. Nothing could be more appropriate, since administrators, teachers, students and their talents, facilities of the school and community resources and attitudes vary so widely not only from state to state, but from town to town or city.

And nothing in the field of education can be more *in*appropriate than refusing to let children learn as much as they can. They can't learn as much as they are capable of in districts that continue to let adult prejudices stemming from the 1930s and 1940s hold them back with slogans which have time and time again been proved invalid, but which are still used to prevent today's children from learning as fast as they can. The resultant waste of time, effort and money, and the boredom and frustration of both pupils and teachers, are incalculable.

As most schools are still set up, in the traditional graded pattern, it seems advisable to accelerate gifted children in the elementary years (K–6) or in junior high. My earlier suggestion that we might abolish junior high was one of those brainstorms creative people get which are sure to shock the general populace, but seventh and eighth grades do provide little besides review of elementary subjects and an orientation toward senior high.

"In seventh and eighth grades I felt kinda useless," a gifted student said. "I was only drifting."

Responsible educators like Ruth Strang ("a good plan seems to be to complete the first three grades in two years and the three junior high grades in two years") support the thesis that valuable time can be saved for good students in the early grades, when they naturally learn the basics faster than average-ability children do, and have to sit around a lot; then when they finally get out of junior high to first or even second year high school—with its wide choice of major academic subjects needed for college, variety of languages, typing, art, music, drama and other electives, vocational exploratory courses and a wealth of extracurricular activities —at a time when social life is more important to the kids than ever before, they don't begin to have time for it all.

Current suggestions for the gifted in high school include Dr. James Bryant Conant's (1966) "give them more work;" as a minimum, four years of math, four years of foreign language, three years of science, four years English and three of social studies, and advanced placement college level courses besides. He also suggests shortening periods so they could take art or music as well as five solids and the required physical education and driver's ed. At the opposite pole is a Los Angeles recommendation (1972) that academic subject requirements be cut and even students planning on college and professional careers—all students— be required to prepare for a trade before they could get a high school diploma.

Vocational education is certainly a good thing, and we should have more of it (only more realistic for *today's* job market), but for gifted students *this* is ridiculous! And the work involved in Dr. Conant's stringent academic requirements might not be too much if implemented in some sort of flexible scheduling or independent study plan, but in the traditional fifty-minute periods with lessons geared to the average mentality there would be too much *wasted* time just sitting in the classroom.

If elementary and junior high schools would offer additional courses (as some do) for gifted children to take in their spare time, such as more than "token" science, typing, several languages and algebra in junior high, then acceleration at this level would not be so necessary; then when gifted boys and girls get to high school they wouldn't have to "give up" typing, speech or a second language. Also, the current emphasis on acceleration in high school *rather than* in the earlier grades would make more sense.

An example of what can be done is San Diego's elementary typing program for the gifted, which began at one school with about fifteen students and has expanded to 34 centers with over 1500 kids. Three teachers travel around with the equipment, and Mrs. Curry, the District Coordinator, says, "You should see the children lined up waiting for their turn!"

Leta Hollingworth, too, said the gifted in elementary schools are wasting their time. Studies over a three-year period showed that a quarter of all children could master all the mental work in half the time, while children of 170 IQ could do all the studies with top marks in about one-fourth of the time they are "compelled" to spend in school.

"They teach themselves to read backwards," she said, "just to fill up the hours."

But, as Jean Piaget says, "the results of a teaching method are much more closely tested and checked when it is destined for use on adults, who have no time to waste . . . than in the case of children, for whom time spent in study is just as precious in fact, but does not appear so in many people's eyes."

10

What Makes a "Gifted" Teacher?

JOHN DRYDEN (17th-century English poet and satirist): *Genius must be born, and never can be taught.*

CARL LINNAEUS (18th-century Swedish professor and botanist): *A professor can never better distinguish himself than by encouraging a clever pupil, for the true discoverers are among them, as the comets among the stars.*

GOETHE (German poet and philosopher, 1749–1832): *A teacher who can arouse a feeling for one good action, for one single good poem, accomplishes more than he who fills our memory with rows on rows of natural objects, classified with name and form.*

AMOS BRONSON ALCOTT (19th-century American philosopher): *The true teacher defends his pupils against his own personal influence. . . . He will have no disciple.*

HENRY ADAMS (writer, editor, historian, in *The Education of Henry Adams,* 1907): *What one knows is, in youth, of little moment; they know enough who know how to learn.*

ROBERT F. DEHAAN (1963): *The teacher's task is more a matter of directing learning, providing materials, and making suggestions to youngsters who are eager and capable of learning rapidly.*

JOHN HOLT (1967): *I would be against trying to cram knowledge into the heads of children, even if we could agree on what knowl-edge to cram, and could be sure that it would not go out of date, even if we could be sure that, once crammed in, it would stay in. For it seems to me a fact that . . . in our struggle to make sense out of life, the things we most need to learn are the things we most want to learn. . . . We want to know for a reason.*

NEIL POSTMAN AND CHARLES WEINGARTNER (1969): *The only way to learn where a kid is "at" is to listen to what he is saying.*

From the student suggestion box of a New York high school (Bel Kaufman's *Up the Down Staircase*, 1964):
List of goods: *1. You're always willing to listen to our side no matter what.*
2. When you don't know something you're not ashamed to say you don't know something.
3. You're not afraid to crack a smile when necessary.
4. You always look happy to see us come in.
Suggestions: *More like you.*

BENJAMIN DE MOTT (in a review of James Herndon's *How to Survive in our Native Land*, *Saturday Review*, September 18, 1971): [*Herndon*] *knows that smart, hardworking, imaginative, decent kids can still, on occasion, be a serious pain in the tail for smart, hardworking, imaginative, decent teachers.*

ANN F. ISAACS (in "A Survey of Suggested Preparation for Teach-ers of the Gifted," *The Gifted Child Quarterly*, Vol. 10, 1966): *Ideally, should the teacher of the gifted be gifted? . . . The key word is* ideally. *. . . With this term . . . the respondents voted in favor of having teachers of the gifted be personally gifted.*

A gifted high school student opinion (1968): *We need less teacher expounding, more seminars, more encouraging the student to go on his own, pursuing the subjects he is interested in. I don't think the average student could handle it—he's too used to being told.*

JOHN CURTIS GOWAN AND CATHERINE BRUCH (in "What Makes a Creative Person a Creative Teacher?" *The Gifted Child Quarterly,* Vol. 11, 1967): *The teacher needs a great deal of energy, self-confident daring, a warm outgoing nature . . . and besides being intelligent and original the teacher must be free of hasty, impatient behavior on the one hand and of anal authoritarianism on the other. With such an order it is not surprising we have so much trouble in getting creative behavior in students.*

CHARLES SILBERMAN (1970): *The free day does not depend on extraordinary talent or genius on the part of the teacher; teachers of every sort—ordinary, garden-variety teachers, not only superior ones—are able to function well in informal classrooms.* [n.b., Mr. Silberman doesn't distinguish gifted pupils or teachers from others.]

SIDNEY P. MARLAND, JR. (1971): *Studies of successful teachers for the gifted typically have dealt with their characteristics and behavior more often than with their specific preparation. In general, the successful teachers are highly intelligent, are interested in scholarly and artistic pursuits, have wide interests, are mature and unthreatened, possess a sense of humor, are more student centered than their colleagues, and are enthusiastic about both teaching and advanced study for themselves.*

GILBERT HIGHET (Professor and writer, classicist, 1954): *Real teaching is not simply handing out packages of information. It culminates in a conversion, an actual change of the pupil's mind.*

GERARD STANLEY (speaking, 1972): *The first thing you need for a gifted program is a good teacher, one who doesn't resent a gifted child. He should have a superior intellect and high energy levels.*

ALVIN EURICH (1969): *. . . the American creative genius must concentrate on making the best possible use of the most gifted teachers now at work or that can be recruited and trained. As* Fortune *magazine has said: "There never can be enough truly* *gifted teachers; the qualities that make for greatness in teaching— like those that make for greatness in any field—are rare."*

J. RICHARD SUCHMAN (Professor of Education, leading exponent of the inquiry teaching method, from a speech in 1962—see James J. Gallagher's *Teaching Gifted Students,* 1965): *The distinguishing characteristic of inquiry as a mode of learning is that it is initiated and controlled by the learner. . . . The problem is to find ways of keeping inquiry alive without discarding the invaluable accumulation of knowledge and theory that is the cultural heritage of each new generation. . . . there are many times and situations when didactic instruction is appropriate and other times when inquiry best serves the needs of the learner.*

JEAN PIAGET (1969, commenting on an experiment in the Malting House School in Cambridge, England, where children of 3–8 were given a laboratory to experiment in all by themselves): *Some form of systematization applied by the adult would perhaps not have been wholly harmful to the pupils. . . . As for those new methods of education that have had the most durable success, and which without doubt constitute the foundation of tomorrow's active school, they all more or less draw their inspiration from a golden mean. [There is] necessity . . . for a surrounding social structure entailing not merely cooperation among the children but also cooperation with adults.*

The paradox here is that there is little doubt as to what makes a good teacher; yet the great majority go right on teaching in the same poor ways.

The controversy is unspoken and unprinted.

Men like James Herndon and Jonathan Kozol teach the *children* instead of the *facts*—and get fired (coast to coast, from San Francisco to Boston). Enthusiastic young (and old) teachers try out new ideas, and parents complain.

The children rarely complain! Many of them in innovative programs are enjoying school for the first time in their lives—*and*
learning how to learn. It's the parents who don't know what's going
on (the ones who don't even take the trouble to find out), and the
administrators (who don't like to listen to the vocal minority of
parents) who are too set in their ways to fight "the necessary
revolution in education."

Charles Silberman reports on the need for change in his massive
best-seller, *Crisis in the Classroom,* and he's talking about *all* children. In over 500 pages he barely mentions the gifted as having
any special needs.

Outstanding teachers like John Holt don't either; the truth is
that if teachers and schools could all be like the ideal that educational philosophers are advocating today, we *might not* need any
special groups or classes or schools for our best students, because
the ideal is an individualized education for *each child.*

No one can quarrel with this philosophy; the only trouble is,
we're a long way from putting it into practice, and we need the
gifted children of *this* generation to—among other things—put it
into practice in the next.

The 1960s are called the Education Decade. Actually, good new
ideas as well as a revived interest in gifted children have been
exploding since the 1950s, with Paul Witty's classic, *The Gifted
Child,* published in 1951 after a long period of educational dol-
drums. When I went to college in the late 1930s we took education
courses because we had to, in order to get teaching jobs. Back in
graduate school in 1969, after raising my family, I had to take
another course, in curriculum, to complete my California State
teaching credential, and I *groaned* at the thought.

The textbook, lectures, and True-False, Multiple-Choice exams
were still dull; the teaching method had changed very little in
thirty years but, oddly enough, the *content* made more sense. My
professor recommended *Education and Ecstasy,* just out that year,
and articles in education and general magazines like the *Phi Delta
Kappan, Changing Times, Look* and the *Saturday Review.* I didn't

share his enthusiasm until I began to read them—they were interesting!

They all said we shouldn't teach by the memorize-and-regurgitate method that some of my college professors and most of my grade-school grandchildren's teachers are still using. I asked my education professor why, since he obviously enjoyed the new ideas, he still gave us those exams on that text-book, and marked us wrong if we didn't say exactly what the book said, word for word.

He *didn't* say, "You're right! I won't do that anymore."

The trouble is, the good ideas are still theories, comparatively rarely used in our schools, and the general public, including many teachers, have scarcely heard of them. The top priority in needs uncovered by the recent Department of Health, Education and Welfare's investigation of the state of education for the gifted and talented was for "better prepared teachers."

Most (though not all) authorities agree that gifted children, because of their unusual mental abilities or special skills, need a different kind of teaching and different kinds of teachers; advanced states like Illinois and Connecticut have already begun to educate teachers in the special field of gifted education, either before or during their service as teachers.

The Office of Education suggests teaching fellowships and in-service training as major needs to "better prepare" these teachers; Professor Gowan pointed out in *Educating the Ablest* (in 1971) that only the University of Georgia, Pennsylvania State, Kent State, George Peabody College, the University of Illinois and the University of Connecticut were prepared to give graduate degrees in gifted education. Dr. Gowan himself runs a summer training course at San Fernando Valley State College, in California, and is instrumental in promoting many classes not only for teachers but for the parents of the gifted. At this writing a few other colleges, including San Diego State (now CSU, San Diego) are preparing teachers for gifted children.

As a first step for improving administrative personnel, the federal government made available $200,000 for a Leadership Training

Institute in Chicago in the summer of 1972. Dr. David Jackson of Illinois, Director, was assisted by Irving Sato (California) and William Vassar (Connecticut). In 1973 and 1974, $400,000 and $500,000 respectively will be available for this and other related projects such as gifted student travel and mentor programs (*i.e.* a professional in his or her field, like a doctor or an artist, is provided for the gifted student to talk to).

The enthusiasm of teachers who *are teaching* the gifted in special programs is a heartening development. Many of them spend their own time and money on courses at local colleges such as the University of California at San Diego extension courses offered by Dr. Larry Meyers, of Temple Beth Israel School, or at summer schools such as those run by the Gifted Students Foundation, Inc., of Texas, headed by Dr. E. R. Simmons.

These teachers band together in associations (with dues!) such as the Association of San Diego Educators for the Gifted which represents 800 teachers of classes for gifted students; they attend workshops and conferences, visit good programs or instructional media centers, and cooperate with parent groups: the San Diego parents association has a thousand members; others in California, like the San Fernando Valley association, have even more. And parents all over the country gave valuable help in the regional hearings conducted by the Department of Health, Education and Welfare for the Report to Congress.

Sharlotte Hydorn, editor of the San Diego Gifted Educators' *Newsletter,* says, "These people are out fighting our battles while we are teaching."

The rapport between parents and teachers is getting better every day, especially where there are special programs for gifted and talented children (not that there aren't *some* cases of emotionally disturbed parents!). But in communities where innovations are frowned on, parents and teachers are still ancient and honorable enemies, and the kids are the ones who suffer.

The other day Arnold Boucher and Marian Williams asked me to visit their gifted cluster at Gage Elementary School: 67 sixth graders, about one-third identified-gifted. For over an hour the children asked the most intimate and searching questions about my book, *Johnny,* which they had all read. They asked about life and death and illness and family relations and writing books, and I answered simply and honestly to the most attentive audience I've ever experienced.

We were talking about courage and sense of humor—they laughed hilariously at Johnny's corniest jokes—when one boy asked seriously, "Did he ever get depressed?"

I knew my answer *mattered* to that boy, though I didn't know why. "Yes, sure," I said. "But he never stayed depressed very long."

"He seems like a pretty neat guy," he said. "I'd like him for a friend."

I came away with the overwhelming conviction that with children like these, we don't have to worry about the future.

Some of the special characteristics teachers of these children should ideally have are discussed by the authorities at the beginning of this chapter. Gowan and Torrance's up-to-date book of readings, *Educating the Ablest,* 1971, is helpful on this and other subjects; and so is Gallagher's *Teaching Gifted Students,* 1965. Norman Mirman, head of the Mirman School for the Gifted in Los Angeles, has a well-regarded article listing "Teacher Qualifications for Educating the Gifted" in *The Gifted Child Quarterly,* Vol. 8, 1964.

Given a teacher with at least one of the qualifications most needed for teaching in this field—enthusiasm!—what are the new, or newly recognized, ways of teaching that will make learning as exciting as it should be? For *all* children?

Few parents and community members who still insist that "what was good enough for me is good enough for the kids today" can also say they *liked* school; very few of the most outstanding men and women of the 20th century, discussed in *Cradles of Eminence,* felt that they *learned* much, if anything, in school.

The wonder is that so many have submitted so docilely for so long to the dullest method of teaching there is. Memorize and repeat, memorize and repeat. . . .

What about the "inquiry method"? It's a commonplace word now in innovative circles; no one bothers to explain it to the many parents and even teachers who don't know exactly how it works, unless they take a course or read up on it. Briefly, you don't *tell* the child, you ask him questions (or have him ask you questions) which lead him to learning for himself. When he learns this way, he *understands* and is more likely to *remember*. In the old lecture or even in the "discussion" method, the teacher directed the thoughts of every child (typically, *en bloc*).

But thoughts don't come that way, which brings us to more of the newly popular theories: teachers should encourage inductive reasoning and divergent rather than convergent thinking. Inductive reasoning starts where we used to leave off—*give* the child some facts, or tell him where to find them, and let him *use* them, think with them as material, formulate his own ideas, as highly creative and mentally gifted children can. As for "divergent thinking," this results in many different ideas, rather than the "one right answer" teachers have been demanding inexorably ever since *I* can remember.

The teacher-directed conclusion doesn't require any thinking at all, usually; it's just rote memory. Everybody who thinks about it admits rote memory isn't much use since knowledge has been doubling every ten years; and as it increases, it often changes as well.

What did you get out of school?

(This is a little exercise in the inquiry method which is supposed to make you realize what I'm driving at without my telling you.)

Silence?

Teachers shouldn't be afraid of silence.

You probably came up with some scattered facts (red, yellow and blue are primary colors, Columbus discovered America, or was it the Vikings?) and dates (1066, 1492, 1776), on the one hand, and some learning skills on the other: how to read, how to write, how to do research in a library, how to type, how to drive a car, or to use lab equipment for scientific experiments, or whatever you "took."

Which have you enjoyed or used the most? The facts or the skills?

Most people will agree that an education should teach us not so much facts as where to find them, and not descriptions or discussions of activities but how to *do* them. Why then do we keep on teaching children to recite facts? Why keep using up valuable skill-teaching time to test students on the contents of a textbook which is either out of date or soon will be, or which, at best, they will forget?

If you're lucky enough to live in an innovative district where no one teaches like this anymore, sing hallelujah. San Diego is generally recognized as being in the forefront of educational reform, and yet a teacher's comment at the bottom of a *junior college* student's test last month read, "Your opinions are valuable. But, when we have an exam on the *textbook,* we're interested in what the *textbook* has to say—right?" (The student's opinion—on how a person feels before giving a speech!—was absolutely valid, but he got a B— instead of an A because he didn't give the textbook writer's feelings!)

The University of Illinois has a self-evaluating *Class Activities Questionnaire* teachers of gifted programs can use to check up on themselves. For information write CAQ, 805 West Pennsylvania, Urbana, Illinois 61801. Nobody sees it but the teacher—a good idea.

If you are a parent, do you know how your children's teachers are teaching them? If you don't like it, what can you do about it?

Maybe you have the answer. I don't know. (A constantly mentioned attribute of a good teacher for the gifted is the nerve to admit that.) Of course, you can always write your Congressmen. That's what sparked the 1971 investigation which disclosed the nationwide neglect of the gifted.

If you're a teacher, and your principal says you have to "cover" a textbook, give tests, make out report cards and keep the kids quiet all the time, what can you do? Only the *great* teachers have any answers, but creative men and women all over the United States, in the old schools against opposition and in the modern schools with support, *are trying*. Some of them are succeeding.

A young blonde from New Jersey, Mary Jane Cyga, teaches advanced English-Social studies, including some gifted kids, at Einstein Junior High School in San Diego; her students have been making educational games and writing and illustrating books for disadvantaged pupils in elementary schools and the children's hospital. Some of the games, like a dial-a-number math game, make use of the principle of immediate feedback, which Miss Cyga told them about.

Dr. Gary Huber is not a secondary school teacher, but he "teaches" teenage students who volunteer to work in Harvard University hospital's Channing Laboratory for Infectious Diseases. They start out doing jobs like washing dishes and running errands, and sometimes end up doing original medical research, as Hunter Nicholas did. This 18-year-old lab helper gave a paper on "The Effect of Experimental Irradiation on the Anti-Bacterial Defense System of the Lung" to the American Federation for Clinical Research in December, 1971.

Like Edmund Bacon, who believed elementary school students could solve city planning problems, Dr. Huber believes that high school students can do useful, original research even though their knowledge of medicine is limited.

"You just need to know how to think," he says.

In another program, an Independent Study student at Pt. Loma High describes a creative use of Pacific Telephone Company's *conference phone call* plan:

"Five of us studied anthropology and read all of Margaret Mead's books. Then our principal made arrangements for a conference phone call. We called her and held a seminar with her. She was in New York and we were in San Diego. Following this I got so excited that I read about the Palauan, Bunyoro, Tiwi, Gururumba, Kapauku and many other societies."

A sophomore high school teacher forced to teach *Silas Marner* didn't just grumble at its irrelevance, as most teachers do; her students put out a newspaper about the town Silas lived in, with (historical) news, editorials, sports pages, letters to the editor, love-lorn columns and comics. They did the same thing with *Julius Caesar* and other "classic" assignments. Another teacher might think of something even better to do with Caesar—the point is to do *something* with it. Of course it's a lot more work, but WORK is more fun than BLAH.

Frank Gross's Enfield High School students, already mentioned, use their spare time, over and above the required subjects, for their social studies laboratory; they furnished and take care of the lab room, give special reports like "The Genesis of a Slum," using community resources; they found a town-owned island in the Connecticut River which they proposed for use as a school wild-life center; and they put out a journal called *Contact*—about "what education can be." Note that in this case the teacher seems hardly necessary, and the term "faculty friend" could well be used as a model in all independent studies projects.

"Jodie" Bruhn, Gifted Counselor at Hale in San Diego, is tackling the widely recognized problem of what happens to gifted students in junior high, where they often get "lost." She got them a special study room, equips it with books, sends the kids to nearby Sunshine School to work with handicapped children, and this year arranged a weekend "retreat" at the School Camp Cuyamaca, for gifted students and some of their parents and teachers; over 120 were there. Imagine a meeting of so many bright young minds under the mountain live-oaks, the sun and the stars, with classes in astronomy, Indian culture, creative dramatics and comparative religion, and "rap sessions" on ecology, war, discrimination, drugs, population, moral standards, law enforcement, books they'd read, and the draft.

In the Creative Dramatics sessions, which I led, we came up—in less than an hour!—with skits for the campfire, including a serious social drama as well as the funny ones we did in other groups.

After I explained how creative dramatics works (each character makes up his own dialog as he acts out the part), the kids worked out their plot—I just asked some good questions, like "What about a social problem we could use for a theme?"

They came up with "people who see someone getting beat up or robbed or even killed but refuse to get involved."

"Where should we set it?"

"A city street."

"Who would be there? What character would you like to be?"

"I'll be the murderer," said—a girl!

Another girl said she'd be the one who was killed, a teacher said he'd be a policeman, three boys decided to be playing ball, somebody's mother offered to be a store-keeper. I asked for volunteers to be a married couple walking by, someone else said she'd be "a nosy neighbor" looking out a window, another a shopper in a hurry.

"What could be the motive for the murder?"

"She's on drugs!"

And so it evolved. The policeman walked by—too early and too late. The boys played ball and did nothing about the girl who was acting so strangely—on drugs. The victim came out of the store and was attacked. No one helped her, then or later as she lay dying. The married couple walked by and argued about it. By the time the policeman strolls by again, the girl is dead.

He questions the boys playing ball, the lady in the window, the store-keeper. Nobody saw anything.

Nobody gets involved.

One of the young men who led a rap session on discrimination used the inquiry method in the extreme form advocated by Neil Postman and Gerald Weingartner. They suggest using only three teacher statements in a class period, otherwise all questions. More statements would subject the teacher to a fine of 25 cents each.

I'd go broke!

Sometimes little comes out of a session like this, the leader told me afterwards, but other times the class explodes, and it's an unforgettable learning experience. One difficulty is that the teacher, in bending over backwards not to admit that there is only "one right answer," may simply pass on to another child for another answer without comment, and leave the child who answered wondering if he is stupid.

This contradicts the strong recommendation of today's educators that children need a good "self-image." We could at least say, without it costing us 25 cents, "That's a good idea!" and *then* ask for others. Children do need praise.

There *is* a "golden mean," agrees Jean Piaget, who has far more influence in the field of education than I; and Dr. Suchman, whose name is linked with the inquiry method, explains in the debate at the beginning of this chapter that statements (lecture, the didactic method) are sometimes more appropriate than questions.

We shouldn't waste the pupil's time in *not* teaching him anymore than we should waste it in the forced feeding of irrelevant facts. All questions could become just as boring as all answers, as a steady diet.

Teachers in training shouldn't believe everything they hear, but on the other hand, there are a lot of good ideas floating around these days, and the inquiry method is one of the best, if not carried to extremes.

As a smart seventh grader told me the other day, her brown eyes twinkling, "You can't believe half what you read in the papers, so I'll believe the half *I* want to!"

If you want to be a good teacher, first, *be informed,* and then *be yourself.* That includes breaking out of the old molds, but it also means not confining yourself in any new ones. Your freedom to teach is as important to your students as their freedom to learn, and most authorities believe that divergent teaching styles are a good thing. The trouble is, teachers haven't been free to teach.

And we've all been so frantically busy teaching the wrong way that we're only beginning to realize how much easier it is to teach—and to learn—in better ways.

If only we are allowed to.

There is hope. My *education textbook* in 1969 actually concluded with, "It is the teachers who experiment in their classes who make the changes that really count. They should be encouraged to do so, for without this experimentation, curricula and courses soon become dreary." (Clark, Klein and Burks, *The American Secondary School Curriculum,* New York, Macmillan Company, 1964.)

But four years after the publication of this text, such a teacher,

Dave Hermanson, conducting such an experiment (the Independent Studies program for gifted students offered at Pt. Loma High School in 1968), in an interview for their school paper, said, "Changing the curricula is like moving a cemetery. The miscellaneous information, scattered and divided data, chaos and incoherence, one text-book, worksheets, Friday movie, Pavlov bell and the 55 minute learning module are so deeply entrenched in the godliness of order, neatness and silence that little change is likely to take place for quite a while."

Within four years, though, there were five of these Independent Studies centers in San Diego, and they have been commended by top national authorities like John Curtis Gowan and William Vassar. With the gifted as pioneers, perhaps some day all students can have this same freedom from the "Pavlov bell."

11

Progress and Prognostications

WILLARD ABRAHAM (1958—the year Russia's "Sputnik" inspired the National Defense Education Act, designed to promote better education for our future scientists and mathematicians so we could win the Space Race): *Hundreds of communities and thousands of parents have made contributions. . . . Cities as widely separated geographically as Portland, Oregon, San Diego, California, University City, Missouri, and Cleveland, Ohio, are in the forefront of a movement constantly increasing its momentum to put the gifted child in the spotlight.* [N.b., this movement had started earlier in the 1950s, perhaps with Paul Witty's classic *The Gifted Child* in 1951; Sputnik provided the motivation needed for national legislation.]

SENATOR JACOB JAVITS (in the *Congressional Record*, January 28, 1969): *In 1958, in response to sputnik, the Congress enacted the National Defense Education Act to identify our most gifted students and to stimulate resources toward meeting the educational needs of these students. However, today, a decade since the passage of NDEA, the Federal effort toward meeting the needs of the gifted and talented has diminished to the point that there is not one single Federal law or program devoting significant resources toward the education of gifted and talented youth. . . . Some States have developed programs. . . . However very few of the over 3 million gifted and talented children of this nation are receiving the special education services they need.*

GLENN T. SEABORG (Chairman, Atomic Energy Commission, in a

141

foreword to Audrey Grost's *Genius in Residence,* 1970): . . . *how many children of unusual intelligence and aptitude do we fail to sift out of the educational mainstream for the special attention that would immediately benefit them and eventually all of us?*

GEORGE I. THOMAS AND JOSEPH CRESCIMBENI (1966): . . . *recommendations for gifted children may appear equally applicable to all children. Ideally this is the case.*

ALVIN C. EURICH (1969): *Show me a school which is not experimenting with new ways of improving education, and I will show you a school which . . . is likely dated for decline. Today good education is largely synonymous with innovative education.*

JAMES HERNDON (July 4, 1967): . . . *frankly I have almost no hope that there will be any significant change in the way we educate our children—for that, after all, would involve liberty, the last thing we may soon expect.*

Committee for Economic Development (in *Innovations in Education,* 1968): . . . *the discovery of new ways to teach children, though a very demanding undertaking, is actually the least difficult part of the task of educational improvement. It is far more difficult to achieve bona fide changes in school programs and organization and to maintain these innovative practices in the face of conservative pressures that resist change and demand a return to the conventional mode.*

ALVIN C. EURICH (1969): . . . *experiments today are testing whether elementary schoolchildren can grasp concepts heretofore thought only suitable for college students; over and over we are finding that our assumptions of what and how children learn are based on what we learned and what the teacher understood a generation ago.*

JEAN PIAGET (1969): *Contemporary society has been profoundly*

*transformed . . . by the work of physicists, chemists and biologists.
. . . the élite formed by such specialists and inventors constitutes
no more than a minute . . . portion of the social body. . . . present-
day intellectual training and public education have turned out to
be singularly ill-adapted to our new needs in the way of training
and recruiting, both in the technical and in the scientific fields.*

GEORGE THOMAS AND JOSEPH CRESCIMBENI (1966): *Special help
programs are needed in rural as well as urban areas. The children
may be classified as poor Mexicans, Puerto Ricans, Chinese, Negroes, or whites, but . . . from this vast reservoir of deprived
children can come the scientists, the authors, the poets, the
musicians and the leaders of tomorrow.*

E. PAUL TORRANCE (in *Gifted Child Quarterly*, 1968): *For some
time I have been experiencing a dawning realization that in the
future we shall have to depend upon creatively gifted members of
disadvantaged and minority cultures for most of our creative
achievements.*

GEORGE LEONARD (1968): [In 2001 A.D. in the Basics Dome in
his utopian Kennedy School] *There are . . . forty learning consoles,
at each of which is seated a child . . . at a keyboard essentially less
complex than an oldfashioned typewriter. . . . almost every symbol
known to human cultures can be produced. . . . Most children go
through the entire basics bank in the four years from age three
through age six.*

MARSHALL MCLUHAN (writer and director of the Center for the
Study of Culture and Technology, University of Toronto, in *This
Book Is About Schools,* 1970): *As the levels of information rise in
the total community . . . very small children have access to very
high learning indeed. . . . quite small children can do top level
research by team methods cooperatively.*

JOHN CURTIS GOWAN (1971): *The development of creativity-stim-*

*ulating curriculum innovations (such as the Williams Cube . . .)
when tied into individualized pupil improvement programs via
computer, will accomplish in a systematic manner what we now do
haphazardly. . . . The next series of revolutionary approaches will
center on the artificial stimulation of intelligence through medical
intervention via drugs, brain-wave modification, high-frequency
electric stimulation of the brain or chemical changes in DNA or
RNA cell structure. Hypnotic and genetic discoveries affecting
intelligence should not be discounted.*

IVAN ILLICH (Director of the Center for Intercultural Documenta-
tion, Cuernavaca, Mexico, in the *Saturday Review,* June 19, 1971):
*I believe that the disestablishment of the school has become in-
evitable.*

In 1945 the Census Bureau thought population might reach 165
million by the year 2000, and college kids were saying, "I wouldn't
want to bring a child into this world!"

What we had were annual baby booms beginning in 1947, and
the Census Bureau's prediction was fulfilled in *ten years.*

"Half our college graduates will have to go into teaching by
1970," a textbook publisher predicted, and in the 1960s the
authorities and the college kids foresaw a catastrophic population
explosion.

Actual births were about 4,313,000 in 1958 and 3,498,000 in
1968. This drastic decline has persisted, with 3,571,000 births in
1969 and 3,718,000 in 1970, *even though these are normal child-
bearing years* (the early twenties) *of the baby boom population!*

The teacher shortage in the 1950s and 1960s, because of the
aforementioned baby booms (1947 ff.), was one of the school's
most serious problems; but suddenly, in 1971, teachers, including
Ph.D.'s, were going begging—100,000 of the 279,000 teachers
prepared in June 1971 would not be needed in September. The
Teacher Corps was a great idea—a bit late. And in view of the

shortage of jobs for trained teachers, the promising teachers' aide program, which is such a help in individualizing instruction for busy teachers trying to handle too many children, could backfire.

At a lunch meeting of the California Association of Childhood Education, a teacher I met was talking about a school in her district which planned to have two master teachers who would direct the activities of lay teacher assistants who would do *all* the teaching! I hope this was only a rumor, and that no such school actually exists.

On the other hand, by 1980 the 1971 figure of 8.5 million college students, according to a Carnegie report, would go up to 13.5 million and to 17.4 million when the baby boom offspring start to college. So then we'd need more teachers—and teachers' aides. However, in light of recent new data, this may very well not happen.

The moral of this round-up of unexpected statistics is that the mere act of making a prognostication, no matter how many authorities concur, does not determine the future; in fact, the opposite state of affairs may ensue, perhaps because people who are concerned about something will do everything they can to prevent it.

At any rate we find ourselves for the first time since this generation can remember with an unemployment problem for teachers. Whether this situation will get better or worse, *I* won't attempt to predict. But no matter what the statistics are, we are going to have to do something about updating our antiquated school systems.

Students of past generations were bored in the monotonous surroundings of a graded classroom, but at least they were trying to learn facts and skills they would need. There was a day, even in this century, when a specialist like a doctor could "cover" most of the medical field in K–12 plus seven years. The knowledge explosion beginning in the 1930s with miracle drugs and atomic fission, for example, has made it increasingly difficult ever since for a general practitioner or a school child to "learn" all there is to know, even in one field. Besides that, what they do learn is soon, sometimes already, outmoded by new kinds of knowledge and the new technological uses to which that knowledge is put.

One of the difficulties schools are running into right now is that by the time they can test something like the teaching machines of the early 1960s something better (?) comes along which they must at least compare. Interestingly, the chief innovations to have survived all the pilot projects are not dependent on machines but on human resources: teachers (e.g. individualization of instruction, the inquiry method and team teaching) and the pupils themselves (independent study, pupils teaching each other).

New teaching styles, human teacher aides, children motivated by the natural desire to learn rather than by tests, grades, and such extraneous requirements: these are our best hope for progress in education. Open schools, classrooms without walls, are also promising, but only because they represent a more open kind of education which can—if necessary—go on in any old building, or in no building at all.

In addition to programs already mentioned throughout this book I will list, for further reference, experiments or established programs that are going on in different parts of the United States; these are not always characterized as "gifted" programs, but it's obvious that the highly involved students *are* gifted (not necessarily by IQ standards) and that these may be good plans to put into operation or adapt for the gifted wherever they seem appropriate. The fact that some of them do work well for all children supports the idea of the gifted as pioneers for experimental programs which may be extended or which will have other "spill-over" values for everyone.

To begin with Paul Witty has an excellent summary of the *history* of gifted programs in this country at the beginning of *The Gifted Child*. To condense:

> 1866: Elizabeth, New Jersey, devised a multiple track system that permitted bright pupils to advance more rapidly than average pupils.
> 1867: a flexible grading and promotion system was introduced in St. Louis.

About 1900: Santa Barbara, California, pupils were placed in groups according to tests.

1912: Individualized instruction was strongly advocated by Frederick Burk of San Francisco, and practiced in other cities.

1920: Special classes for the gifted pupil were formed in Los Angeles, Cleveland, and Rochester, New York.

1930: At the White House Conference on Child Health and Protection it was estimated that there were 1½ million pupils of superior intelligence in the United States who varied so much from the average that they required special education. An investigator reported that only 40 cities in 23 States had schools and classes for such pupils and only about 4000 children were enrolled in all of these. (Cf. figures in 1971 Report to Congress.)

In my list of current programs I will begin with one of the oldest:

Cleveland (Ohio) Major Work Classes. See Willard Abraham, p. 74.

Portland, Oregon, John Adams High School. A student-directed, problem-solving experiment in secondary education. See Charles Silberman, pp. 364–369.

New York, N. Y., Harlem Prep. Successful learning for former public school drop-outs to prepare for college.

St. Louis, Missouri, Visitation-Holy Ghost and St. Ann's Catholic schools. Nongrading, independent study and other programs. See *The Catholic Digest,* October, 1971.

Washington, D.C., Coolidge High School's *Project Catalyst.* Junior chemistry students spend summer doing research at The American University and other college labs.

U. S. International University, which has campuses in Hawaii, England, Colorado and San Diego, offers a "middle college" which combines the last two years of high school and first two of college.

Newton, Massachusetts, High School and Murray Road Annex. Students pursue learning outside school. See Silberman, pp. 356–64.

Chula Vista, California. Year-round school (45–15 plan) in operation since July 1971; also continuing architectural design development for over ten years. See my *Creative Teaching* for architecture, including photos and floor plans.

Burton C. Tiffany is superintendent of the elementary schools, year round program.

Pittsburgh, Pennsylvania, Colfax School, gifted Junior Workshop, grades 1–3 and Senior Workshop, 3–6. Half day in workshop in major subjects; regular classes (art, music, physical education, library) in heterogeneous groups. See Hedwig O. Pregler, *Education,* Vol. 80, No. 3, November 1959.

New York, N. Y. Hunter College has nationally known gifted schools, both elementary and high school.

Decatur, Illinois, Decatur-Lakeview High School, independent study. A class in the problems of independent study and state-required physical education are the only "requirements." Four years to 1970 proved successful.

Portland, Oregon, John Marshall High School. See *Individualized Learning Through Modular-Flexible Programming,* by its principal, Gaynor Petrequin, New York, McGraw-Hill, 1968.

Silver Spring, Maryland, John F. Kennedy High School. Students intern in government and other Washington, D.C., community affairs.

Philadelphia, Pennsylvania, Parkway Program. No school building at all, courses conducted in community facilities.

North Dakota's New School approach. See *Newsweek,* May 3, 1971.

Ocracanoke, North Carolina. 68 students grades 1–12 are doing well in a new one-room school—ungraded.

Colorado Springs, Colorado. 40 percent unscheduled time.

Bronx, New York, High School of Science.

Louisville, Kentucky, The Lincoln School. A secondary school for the exceptionally talented but culturally and economically deprived. See Marvin J. Gold, "Kentucky's Lincoln School for Disadvantaged Gifted Youngsters," in Gowan and Torrance, *Educating the Ablest,* 1971.

Palo Alto, California. A variety of programs for the gifted. The proximity of Stanford University and its facilities leads to some outstanding innovative programs like Patrick Suppes's work with computers. Mrs. Ruthe Lundy, Coordinator, reports elementary pupils doing well when they take junior or senior high courses.

Venice, California (Los Angeles City Schools). Westminster Avenue School gifted children elected a mayor and city council and planned an ideal community. See *Los Angeles Times,* Sunday, July 5, 1970—Real Estate Section!

Brooklyn, New York, Talent School, P.S. 260. See *Instructor,* February 1971.

New York, N. Y., Elementary P.S. 158. Free reading, and P.S. 134, individually prescribed instruction in math. See *Parents',* September, 1970.

Winnetka, Illinois, Junior High. Independent study since 1964, originally for gifted only, turns out to be good for slow learners and underachievers.

Melbourne High School, Florida. See Janet Whitmire, "The Independent Study Program at Melbourne High," *Phi Delta Kappan,* Vol. 47, September, 1965.

Oneonta, New York, the Catskill Area Project arranges for pupils in rural areas to take seminars at the State College, summers and Saturdays of the school year.

San Diego, California, has a wide variety of gifted programs for over 7000 identified gifted students, under Elementary and Secondary Coordinators, with two District Resource Teachers working full-time. Dr. Hermanson, Secondary Coordinator, reports that of 3772 identified gifted junior and senior high school students, 2999 are in full-year programs and 433 more have been in one semester or special classes; the elementary programs have a similar record, with well over 80 percent of the identified gifted being served. (Nationally, according to the Report to Congress, "one-third or more of the known gifted receive no special instruction of any kind.")

Elementary clusters at central schools in San Diego include a number of gifted with regular students; junior high schools have seminars and various plans for outstanding students including independent study at O'Farrell, Collier, Hale, Memorial and others; high schools have advanced and honors classes and the independent study centers, described earlier. Patrick Henry High School is the most innovative for total student population under the NASSP Model Schools Program.

An outstanding feature of San Diego gifted education is the Pupil Study Center, staffed by a clinical psychologist, a psychiatric social worker, and a counseling psychiatrist available at all grade levels to gifted children with problems, and their parents.

States which are outstanding for their programs include Connecticut, under its Consultant, William Vassar. In 1966 Connecticut had only one college course in gifted education; now there are three graduate level programs, and four other colleges have course sequences. In 1967 only four school districts had programs for the gifted; now 62 districts have programs which include an old college campus used as a talent retrieval center for disadvantaged students; a mountain top for the highly gifted in earth and space science (see "Talcott Mountain Science Center for Student Involvement," by Donald P. La Salle and George C. Atamian in Gowan and Torrance, 1971); a renovated synagogue to serve as a high school center for pupils outstanding in the creative arts from 18 surrounding school districts; and an ice cream factory which has become a theater for Inner City kids, with the help of June Havoc and Harry Belafonte.

"It's a good idea to mix the Terman-type kids, high creative producers, the talented in the arts, and bright underachievers. They work well together," Vassar says. "They turn each other on."

He suggests using talent-interest areas to get children involved in the academic area, and advocates the utilization of community resources.

Any mountains, islands or ice-cream factories in your bailiwick?

The Report to Congress (Volume 2, Background Papers) describes Connecticut, California, Illinois and Georgia provisions for the gifted as models. Georgia's Governor's Honors Program includes an eight-week residential program for 400 high school juniors and seniors talented in art, music, drama, or with high mental ability. (North Carolina has a similar program.)

Illinois builds its program around a large number of enthusiastic consultants who are available to help schools that establish their own individual programs throughout the state. They have just completed an extensive evaluation, and interested educators may write Robert Hardy, Director, Illinois Gifted Program, 1020 So. Spring, Springfield, Illinois 62706, for details. James Gallagher, a former leader in Illinois, is now at the Frank Porter Graham Child Development Center, University of North Carolina, Chapel Hill, N. C., which handled the statistics for the Report to Congress.

Articles in newspapers and magazines and the above examples of innovative programs are, of course, "news." We seldom hear about any of the great majority of schools that haven't changed for several generations, nor about what is *not* being done for our best students.

"When you've seen one, you've seen 'em all" is an apt description of the typical American classroom most of us remember: 30 or more pupils cooped up in one colorless cell from 8 or 9 to 3 o'clock at an age when children are at their most rambunctious. And there is only one teacher to keep them *quiet,* a task that interferes greatly with teaching—and learning. In secondary schools the kids can move around some, and look at different teacher-faces, but discipline remains the number one priority.

In ghetto schools such as those described in *The Way It Spozed To Be, Up the Down Staircase, The Blackboard Jungle* or *Death At An Early Age,* it has become increasingly difficult to maintain any order at all. This is one of the new problems in America that *demand* solutions we were able to get along without—however badly—in the first half of the century.

Technological changes creating new kinds of jobs and careers and eliminating old ones; the spiralling increase of knowledge; inflationary costs of all school materials and services; earlier maturing of our young people (in some ways!); the doubling and redoubling of property and other tax burdens at a time when many school buildings are need to replace those built in the 1920s and 1930s; the closing of many Catholic and other private schools with survivors excelling in innovative education; recent court decisions declaring the financing of education by local taxes unconstitutional; a new and desirable interest in vocational and career education which *could,* however, evolve at the expense of the academic—perhaps above all, the controversy over integration by busing as opposed to compensatory education programs: these and many more current conditions must be taken into consideration today. We can't dispense education from the same old stand.

History provides plenty of examples of the "radical" experimentation that leads to our most conservative institutions. It also provides case studies in the biographies of the gifted men and women who made those experiments, and were often persecuted in return. The average citizen has always resisted change, just as he does today. That's why we propose using the gifted of this generation to work out the changes we need to make in this decade of educational transition.

Gifted students like to experiment; in most cases, their parents, sometimes gifted themselves, are overwhelmingly in favor of innovative programs, whereas the average parent often opposes any new methods of handling his children. I can just hear the wail that would go up across the land if elementary schools stopped sending home report cards with grades on them, but who needs them? In high school, maybe, because of the set-up for getting into college; in college, maybe, as recommendations for graduate schools and careers; but why in elementary school? If we could get rid of them there, we might get kids motivated by the fun of learning, and *then* we wouldn't need them at any level.

The chief complaint you hear from parents of the gifted is, "When are you going to do something for *my* child?"

They are justified. The mandated Report to Congress in 1971 described an intensive 11-month nationwide study which concluded that programs for the gifted were "practically nonexistent" for minority group children and serve "only a very small percentage of the gifted and talented population generally."

Only 21 states have any legislation to provide for these "deprived" children, and those, in many cases, show merely "token intent."

"Identification of the gifted is hampered . . . by apathy and even hostility among teachers, administrators, guidance counselors and psychologists," it declares (and we knew it all the time).

In 1966, a survey of the states disclosed that about one-third indicated their state boards of education had policies against spending special education funds (which cover both physically or mentally handicapped and gifted) for the education of the gifted!

There *is* some federal money for disadvantaged-gifted programs, and for demonstrating innovative plans, which is not being used. Federal funds under PL-89-10, Titles I, III and V are available but have been utilized by only seventeen states and Puerto Rico; most of these use very little. States with the more outstanding programs generally use state money.

The list of innovative and established programs above doesn't of course include all such programs; no doubt I've left out some very good ones, and I'd be glad to hear about them. There are also some that aren't so good.

As John Hersey, author of the unforgettable *Hiroshima,* says in *Educational Leadership* 13, January 1956, "Talent is elusive, fragile, manifold, fast-moving, luminous, tantalizing, and incredibly beautiful, like aurora borealis on a cool September night. Who would give a weatherman a bag of money and tell him to go out and catch some northern lights? . . . Our uncertainty about exactly how to develop talent is only one part of the greatest unsolved problem in American education—the problem of how to help every child realize his maximum potential . . . the problem of individual differences."

The Report to Congress (1971) agrees: "The major thrust in American education today is to free all students to learn at their own pace—and to place on them more responsibility for their education."

The chief obstacle to this, also recognized in the report, is the unwillingness of faculty members to *free* gifted students for that learning. A teacher who excuses a student from his class may feel he is admitting that what *he* has to teach is not important. Gifted teaching personnel and students should be not only tactful but considerate; some days it *is* important!

Another question is, are students of average ability suited to such programs too? Probably not, since it is not only a matter of ability but also of desire. Anti-gifted adults often say anyone who wants to should be able to be in a special program. Amen. I agree. But children who don't learn easily don't enjoy it as much as those who do, and—unless "pushed" by adults—would usually rather not "read all that much" or do all that extra WORK. Whether reading a book is work or fun depends largely on how well you can read, at any given level.

On the other hand, as Alvin Eurich says, when students move at their own rates the whole class, slow students as well as fast ones, are likely to learn much more. Often the underachieving bright child needs only to learn to read better in order to take his place with the others.

Some experimental programs, generally those characterized by *extreme* permissiveness, such as the school of arts Walt Disney endowed at his death, will continue to be not unjustly criticized; some (not all) of the "free schools," contain irresponsible teacher-leaders who condone drug abuse and promiscuity; lazy "students" who take advantage of the freedom *not* to learn; and boys and girls who fail to accomplish anything within a program because they weren't ready for it to begin with. Unfortunately, many otherwise successful programs fail because of community opposition or lack of funds. It's hard, as Leta Hollingworth said, to get money for our most potentially useful citizens.

"Why endow the gifted?" critics ask. "What do they need money for?"

Chiefly, for personnel. For qualitatively different programs, classes that either include or are composed of exceptional children should be limited in size, which means more teachers are needed. State laws often require this for handicapped children; classes for gifted need not be so small as classes for blind or orthopedically disabled, but a load of no more than 15 or 20 pupils per teacher is advisable, and this is required by some school districts.

Teacher aides and assistants, paraprofessionals, resource teachers, coordinators and consultants are helpful in ways already mentioned. Guidance and psychology personnel, including psychometrists for testing, are also needed. Teacher training, especially inservice classes, are indispensable with innovative programs, and these must also be evaluated, although as a lay critic I'd say evaluation is often overdone; it sometimes goes hand in hand with bureaucracy. The paper storm may be a snow job.

Books and other enrichment materials and money for special

field trips and laboratory equipment are some other expenses; but 43 times as much is spent on the handicapped pupil as on the gifted, in federal funds, and of the states, only Connecticut spends as much on the gifted as on other exceptional children.

Money spent on outstanding children may be returned to the public in many ways: for instance, acceleration programs mean gifted children spend fewer years in school, which saves tax money (as much as $1700 per pupil per year in New York City); more productive and talented men and women, as Ruth Martinson points out, with statistics, in the Report to Congress, will *pay* more taxes.

Beth Smith, president of the San Diego Association for Gifted Children, has a pet statistic. "We could build a special school for the gifted and provide $250 a year each for 500 students for $3 million," she says. "That's what it costs to build one mile of freeway."

This could be the first public school for gifted children in the west, although New York and other eastern schools have proved successful. It would have the cooperation and could use facilities of the University of California at San Diego.

Such a school is a special dream of David Hermanson's, for grades 7–12, and he and Cecil Munsey have written it up in their *Working Paper 8, A Conceptual Framework for a High School for Gifted Students.* Or, he suggests, a central library and learning center might serve the gifted from all the schools in the district. It could be staffed by resident or visiting experts in a variety of fields, and would help more students for less money.

$3 million, anyone? Or even a million?

The payoff for such programs usually comes when the kids grow up, but it can come even sooner. Involvement in community life and the solution of community problems are a frequently advocated activity for our most creative school children. Some ways have been mentioned already in which teen-age or even small children have contributed to our society. Did you know that Louis Braille started work on his system of reading for the blind when he was 12, and finished at 16?

S. I. Hayakawa, one of the most distinguished scholars of our times, says schools cannot substitute for real life; that's why they have been so boring. He agrees that even small children can do many helpful things, and talks about a friend of his who had a great idea for New York City's 400,000 high school students. They could clean up the city, plant trees, direct traffic, deliver mail, take care of kids so their mothers could get off relief, tutor elementary school children, help the old, retarded and crippled.

He advocates a national Youth Service Corps that boys and girls could join as soon as they graduated from high school, like the Peace Corps or the Civilian Conservation Corps of the Depression, or Vista. We can hope the Teacher Corps will be needed, and that military service will not. We can dream that a great army of youth workers will clean up and rebuild our cities, towns and countryside, and help the poor and suffering in every part of the world.

All of our children can do this, all of our children have gifts; but we will need more and more the special gifts of the leaders, the problem-solvers—

And the dreamers.

12

Conclusions

The research in education for the gifted is so rich that all the interesting studies and hardworking leaders in the field can't possibly be included in one book. Unfortunately, their well-documented evidence and reasonable recommendations have been ignored for years.

Do we really want egg-crate classrooms? Boring textbooks? "Students" who hate to study? Teachers who aren't allowed, or can't find the time, to teach?

Will the new programs that make kids *want* to learn be used more widely—or will they be stamped out by people who don't understand the meaning of intellectual curiosity because it was so rare in the schools they went to?

Will the recent report to Congress on the "nationwide neglect" of our future leaders result in more than token remedies for that neglect? Or will all that work result in another sputtered-out "Sputnik" effort, as the 1958 enthusiasm and the promising "Project Talent" had by the mid 1960s?

Among the positive gains, the Office of Education has just appointed, for the first time, a full-time chief in charge of gifted and talented education at the federal level. His name is Harold Lyon—he's young and enthusiastic, and he will be assisted by Deputy Jane Case Williams, who engineered the two-volume report to Congress: *Education of the Gifted and Talented.*

In a second Javits Bill, Congressional leaders are recommending the allocation of $80 million for gifted and talented children and youth. In the past, most legislation at both state and federal levels has voted money for "exceptional children," which includes the handicapped as well as the gifted, and this resulted in the federal funds being spent 43 to 1 in favor of the physically handicapped and 28 to 1 in favor of the educationally handicapped.

The sum of $80 million for the gifted, divided among all the states as $60 million of it is slated to be, is hardly a fortune, but enthusiastic leaders all over the country are just hoping the bill will be passed. It was introduced in the Senate by Senator Javits March 21, 1972; whether, as you read this, this particular bill (S.3382) has been passed or not, such legislation should be supported by every parent, teacher and administrator who is interested in better education for our best students, who will be in positions of influence within the next twenty years.

S.3382 is co-sponsored by Senators Harrison A. Williams, Jr. (D, New Jersey), J. Glenn Beall, Jr. (R, Maryland), Alan Cranston (D, California), Abraham A. Ribicoff (D, Connecticut), James B. Pearson (R, Kansas), Claiborne Pell (D, Rhode Island), Richard S. Schweiker (R, Pennsylvania), Ted Stevens (R, Alaska), Adlai E. Stevenson III (D, Illinois) and John Tunney (D, California). Letters to these or other Senators should be addressed to the Senate Office Building, Washington, D. C. 20510.

Parent organizations have done a great deal already to influence legislators. Thousands of parents from many states were behind the over 415 parents who wrote letters for the Department of Health, Education and Welfare's regional Advocate Survey, on which the Report to Congress was based. Beverly King, President of the California Parents for Gifted, served on a panel of national leaders who acted in an informal advisory capacity, along with leaders from the Ford Foundation and other friends of education in the business world.

What if the students themselves—those who want or are already enjoying a more challenging education—should write their Congressmen and their state legislatures? This is something even very young gifted students could do, and with the voting age now lower, youth cannot be ignored.

"The politicians are beginning to come around to visit us," a boy in high school told me the other day. "They didn't bother with us before!"

We need to swell the numbers of interested citizens if we are to make permanent gains this time.

But these same students have an even more important responsibility to boys and girls in our future schools. Pilot programs are evaluated and tested by follow-up studies; such studies have already, in some of the long-established plans like the Cleveland Major Work Classes, demonstrated success.

Freedom to learn is going to depend on how well these pioneers do learn when they "don't have to." There's no question about the enthusiasm with which most gifted boys and girls tackle subjects they're interested in, the books they'll read and the work they'll do. But extreme permissiveness on the teacher's part in introducing them to new areas of knowledge may result in their interests remaining limited; refusal to accept any of the disciplines that learning itself imposes will result in a shallow education.

"Genius is one percent inspiration and 99 percent perspiration" is still true. You can't make a work of art without the work—

But work can be fun!

If we free our children from artificial restrictions, such as textbooks to be "covered," and irrelevant motivations, such as grades, and then if even *some of them* accept this as the freedom *not* to learn, those follow-up studies are going to make great ammunition for the exponents of coercive education.

The responsibility is the teacher's even more than the pupil's. No matter what kind of education you advocate, teachers still have to teach. But students still have to study, too.

So what are the major problems in providing a better education for our best students? As I see it after this survey of the field, what is needed most of all is:

1. Community backing. This has always been the problem, but it could be the solution.

2. Administrative backing; you can't have a program without the support of the principal of the school. Principals have a great

deal of power in our system of education, and that should be a good thing, since communities differ in their needs and resources, and direction by a distant agency would be intolerable to most Americans (even Democrats!). However, this means that while a principal can provide, or appoint, the creative leadership necessary for outstanding new programs, he or she can also smother any sparks of enthusiasm directed toward improving "the way it's always been done." And principals are extremely sensitive to parents, for which we can blame—or thank?—a gifted guy named Alexander Graham Bell.

3. Teachers sympathetic with bright students and prepared to teach them in better ways: this was a top priority in the recommendations made by the Office of Education, which included provision for inservice and special training and degrees in gifted education as well as the selection of teachers who are naturally suited to this work.

4. Dissemination of ideas: until very recently states and even school districts struggled alone, with much duplication of effort. Some examples of recent improvement on this score include the formation of "The Steering Committee of the National Coordinating Council for the Education of the Gifted and Talented" in New York City in December 1971. For a good account of its objectives see the Spring 1972 Newsletter of the Gifted Children Research Institute, formed in April 1971 by Carol Wolverton and Alan Rogers; their address is Suite 4-W, 300 West 55th Street, New York, N. Y., 10019.

Also, at the University of Virginia, Virgil Ward, a leader in the field for many years, has embarked on a study involving leaders of gifted programs all over the country. Best of all, The Office of Education has finally established that special Office of Gifted and Talented Education under director Harold Lyon and Deputy Jane Case Williams. This office, at 7th and D streets, N.W., Washington, D. C. 20202, will act as a clearinghouse for information.

5. Money! This may seem a long way down the list, but there are things money can't buy as well as things you can't have without it. Many gifted students *have* come successfully through our

schools, and most of them attribute this to a few outstanding teachers. As far as general funds are concerned, the community has, in the past at least, backed our schools, and superintendents have, on the whole, run them in a businesslike way. Very little, though, has ever been spent on the gifted, and the Report to Congress documents this fact.

Currently the community is not too happy about *anything* that costs extra money, and that's understandable. I'm a taxpayer myself, *and it hurts.*

But why have we only barely begun to tap all the community resources which are available either free or at low cost? For examples, see my *Creative Teaching,* 1971, Chapter 5, "Help from the Community." A book could be written on this subject alone, including expert volunteer personnel from business and the arts, and local colleges; and "schools without buildings" programs— like the Philadelphia Parkway Program—which use community facilities. Initial expenses in such projects should pay off in the long run; individual teachers with initiative often run programs that not only don't cost anything, but even make money, like selling original Christmas cards (one elementary school made and sold 4000) or books of poetry written and illustrated by the kids.

Also, better education for our best students can *save* money. This could come about in several ways already touched on:

1. By *acceleration,* the elementary and secondary education of able students can be accomplished in at least one to three years less time per student. This would save on teachers' salaries, number of classrooms needed, materials and administrative expenses. Many studies show that acceleration does not harm pupils or that it is of benefit. Claims that it does harm are based on individual cases and emotional prejudices, which often stem from the educational climate *c.* 1930–1950; some authorities include the 1920s. In my husband's and my experience as pupils in the 1920s in Washington, D. C. and California, and as parents in the 1940s in Maine, the opposition got worse. But perhaps geography has something to do with it, too.

2. The better education of more of our outstanding students

would result in their becoming more productive members of our society; as such they would pay more than the average share of the tax load. As Ruth Martinson points out in Volume 2 of the Report to Congress (*Education of the Gifted and Talented*) the difference between average lifetime high school and fifth-year college income is $246,000 (Bureau of Census, *Digest of Educational Statistics,* 1970). The income tax on this difference, in a conservative 25 percent bracket, would be $61,500.

Yet right now states with the *best* programs for the gifted spend less than $100 per year per pupil above the regular school program; $92 is the figure based on model districts in California, Florida, New York, Texas and Wisconsin. If we spent $250 a year, a more reasonable amount which would still be far less than is spent on the physically handicapped ($1729.) and retarded ($1291.), the special education of all the different kinds of gifted students throughout their entire school career would cost $3000 per pupil (*if* he attended twelve years), but this same pupil would (and might not otherwise) "repay" $61,500 or more—in taxes based on increased earning power.

Having said all this to persuade anyone who cares that much about money, I must add that what most of us who are fighting for them really care about is the kids. A truly deserving minority— in all colors.

3. Bored geniuses and undeveloped leaders and creative artists are potential dropouts, delinquents, criminals, or anyhow welfare recipients! All these cost a lot of money—and cause a lot of misery.

Education, as almost every outstanding educator since Plato has said, should above all be aimed at the development of virtue. An exception would be Machiavelli's instructions to *The Prince,* but he is in such a minority that his name has become synonymous with "evil."

Plato said, "Education makes good men."

Locke said, " 'Tis virtue then, direct virtue, which is the hard and valuable part to be aimed at in education."

Many more such quotations could be added, and studies show

that gifted children tend to be good, to be generous, compassionate and honest. Is an educational system in which such children are held back, frustrated, deprived of their natural joy in learning and producing going to make them better citizens? And should we continue to waste so much of their valuable *time?*

A good point often made is that their presence in classrooms with other children is helpful and stimulating. More authorities agree that part of their time may well be spent in regular classrooms, that they can tutor slower learners, to their mutual benefit, as Debbie Krolik enjoyed doing at Sunshine School.

But authorities also agree that gifted, talented and creative children are stimulating to *each other,* and should spend a substantial part of their time with their true peers. When we talk about "peer groups" and "peer pressure," we tend to assume that children of the same chronological age are peers, since this is the way our schools are arranged. But Funk and Wagnalls *Standard College Dictionary* says *peer* means "an equal, as in natural gifts or in social rank"—a most "undemocratic" definition!

Some of the highly gifted, especially those who live in small towns, succumb to social pressures because they wouldn't have *any* friends otherwise; some simply cannot bring themselves to conform and are lonely and unhappy. Some well-adjusted children, especially if they have understanding parents or teachers, manage to educate and entertain themselves, and maintain their individuality; they may become social leaders as well.

The dissemination of information such as techniques, programs, and available funds for gifted students is also especially needed in the less populated areas. Many of our large cities are not only developing outstanding programs of their own; educators are hopping planes to share ideas with other advanced states and cities. But in too many small towns and rural areas some of the nicest little kids in town are getting a rough deal. If their teachers and school boards have even heard of any new ways of educating good students, they're dead set against them.

These are the children, along with the unrecognized talented and gifted hidden in the ghettoes and slums of the cities, who are most in need of our help. Their only advocates are, *sometimes,* their parents, who get nothing but abuse for their concern.

The gifted in the ghettoes rarely have even these natural advocates. But a natural-born leader is hard to put down. Many people think of all members of poor or deprived minorities as lazy, "shiftless," or unambitious simply because the *average* members of these communities find it hard to rise above their disadvantages. But the gifted want to "move up," to get out of the ghetto. They are not shiftless or unambitious but *hungry* for success.

If only we give them a chance.

Unfortunately, colleges that accept any black or brown student on a *nonselective* basis, as some do under the Educational Opportunities Program, may be doing these communities a disservice. It doesn't help anyone's self-image if he fails, and there are too many other minority students who have the qualifications needed for success. We must *find* them, early in their elementary school careers, or sooner, and *prepare* them: for college if they are academically talented or for an art or a trade or a skill.

We should "develop total talent," says Joseph Rice, Chief of the Bureau of Special Education in California in his comprehensive 1970 book, *The Gifted.* "Create a talent pool" of children gifted in all the ways there are: mentally superior, highly creative, talented in one of the performing arts, mechanically or physically or socially gifted or (usually) a combination of these.

"The public has never bought isolation for Terman-type kids," as Connecticut's William Vassar says, "but once you start broadening the concept you get more public support."

The old objection of special education for gifted children as undemocratic may finally be scotched if we find the outstanding members of all communities and *find them as young as they must be found* if 80 percent of a person's intelligence is developed by age 8—the latest estimate. We must provide preschool education for those whose parents can't or won't, and give them the special attention and encouragement they need during their years of compulsory education. We make them go to school, presumably to learn. The least we can do is to let them learn while they are there.

I wish I knew what we could do about the all-time problem of the otherwise good and kindly Americans whose compassion reaches out to the handicapped, but who resent bright children. If we broaden our definition of who *is* gifted, though, we are going to invade just about every family in the land.

Parents are noted for being proud of their own offspring, for whatever reason, and I don't think much of any parent who isn't. Somebody else's kids being considered smarter is what seems to be hard to take, so the more parents we get involved by identifying *their* children as outstanding, the more support we will have for gifted education, as Dr. Vassar says.

This new concept is going to run into some opposition, of course, from an old guard accustomed to fighting for the neglected kids with the high IQs; we haven't won our battle for *them* yet, either. But most of today's leaders in the field —Torrance, Gowan, Gallagher, Sato, Vassar, Martinson, Ward, Hermanson and many more—know that geniuses turn up in the most unlikely backgrounds, and that the IQ tests we've been using are better suited to the kids in the high socioeconomic communities, on the whole. This doesn't mean we haven't found kids with IQs of 200 in all walks of life and at all economic levels. Nor does it mean that we don't still need programs designed especially for the mentally gifted at high cutoff points. Appropriate programs should be devised for all types of giftedness.

Giftedness?

The terms we use are so seldom satisfactory. Gifted kids don't like to be called gifted kids. Obviously, *superior* is out, and so is *élite,* except as a joke, like when they call themselves *weird. Able* is stuffy, *smart* is apt to be followed by *aleck; bright* isn't quite so bad.

Exceptional would have been passable, but it somehow got identified more with the retarded and handicapped, as a euphemism, and it works well for that purpose. So these other "special" children are still looking for a name. The Department of Health,

Education and Welfare has placed them under the supervision of the Bureau of the Handicapped, and this causes mixed emotions on the national scene.

"Every time I hear the gifted being called handicapped I feel outraged," says Ann Isaacs, editor of the *Gifted Child Quarterly*.

But Bill Vassar says this is the way to go if you want people to give them any money. It worked in Connecticut.

Others write articles to show how gifted children are, in fact, "handicapped" by their unusual brains or skills, or "deprived" of the kind of education they need.

Why couldn't we use the term *leaders*?

The American people have pretty good feelings about leadership, and it would cover "mentally gifted minors" (MGM is the California word), champion athletes and creative artists or skilled mechanics and craftsmen, as well as political, social, professional and industrial leaders.

We could have leadership programs rather than gifted programs; kids chosen for them, like officers in extracurricular activities, would be admired rather than resented; age-group pressure would be put to good use rather than used as a weapon to destroy talent and self-confidence.

And *all* children would be motivated to develop any potential talents; the "underachievers," the "average," the "disadvantaged" and the physically or educationally handicapped as well as those who seem to be born with a golden spoon in their mouths. Indeed, we all know how often a handicapped child will do much more than the one for whom everything comes too easily.

Utopian? No, possible. *And we are headed in that direction.* This is the most hopeful sign of permanent progress in the history of special education for the children who want it most:

The ones who love to learn.

Bibliography

Books

Abraham, Willard. *Common Sense About Gifted Children*. New York: Harper and Brothers, 1958.

Ames, Louise Bates. *Is Your Child In The Wrong Grade?* New York: Harper & Row, 1967.

Aschner, M. J. and Charles E. Bish, eds. *Productive Thinking in Education* (revised). Washington, D. C.: National Education Association, 1968.

Barbe, Walter B., ed. *Psychology and Education of the Gifted*. New York: Appleton-Century-Crofts, 1965.

Beadle, Muriel. *A Child's Mind*. New York: Doubleday, 1970.

Beck, Joan. *How to Raise a Brighter Child*. New York: Trident Press, 1967.

Birmingham, John, ed. *Our Time Is Now*. New York: Praeger, 1970.

Black, Hillel. *The American Schoolbook*. New York: William Morrow, 1967.

Boorstin, Daniel J. *The Sociology of the Absurd*. New York: Simon & Schuster, 1971.

Bricklin, Barry and Patricia M. *Bright Child—Poor Grades*. New York: Delacorte Press, 1967.

Brown, B. Frank. *The Nongraded High School*. Englewood Cliffs, N. J.: Prentice-Hall, 1963.

Bruner, Jerome S. *The Process of Education*. Cambridge, Mass.: Harvard University Press, 1960.

Clark, Leonard H., Raymond L. Klein and John B. Burks. *The American Secondary School Curriculum*. New York: Macmillan, 1964.

Coleman, James S. *et al. Equality of Educational Opportunity*. Washington, D. C.: National Center for Educational Statistics, U. S. Government Printing Office, 1966.

Conant, James B. *The American High School Today.* New York: McGraw-Hill, 1959.

————. *The Comprehensive High School.* New York: McGraw-Hill, 1967.

DeHaan, Robert F. *Accelerated Learning Programs.* Washington, D. C. (now in New York): Center for Applied Research in Education, 1963.

Dodson, Fitzhugh. *How to Parent.* Los Angeles: Nash Pub. Corp., 1970.

Engelmann, Siegfried and Therese. *Give Your Child a Superior Mind.* New York: Simon & Schuster, 1966.

Eurich, Alvin C. *Reforming American Education.* New York: Harper & Row, 1969.

———— ed. *High School 1980: The Shape of the Future in American Secondary Education.* New York: Pitman, 1970.

Evans, E. Belle, Beth Shub and Marlene Weinstein. *Day Care: How to Plan, Develop and Operate a Day Care Center.* Boston, Mass.: Beacon Press, 1971.

Fine, Benjamin. *Your Child and School.* New York: Macmillan, 1965.

————. *Underachievers.* New York: E. P. Dutton, 1967.

Fliegler, Louis A., ed. *Curriculum Planning for the Gifted.* Englewood Cliffs, N. J.: Prentice-Hall, 1961.

Gallagher, James J. *The Gifted Child in the Elementary School.* Washington, D. C.: National Education Association, 1959.

————. *Teaching the Gifted Child.* Rockleigh, N. J.: Allyn & Bacon, College Division, 1964.

————. *Teaching Gifted Students: A Book of Readings.* Boston: Allyn & Bacon, 1965.

Galton, Francis. *Hereditary Genius, an Inquiry into its Laws and Consequences.* New York: World Pub. Co., 1962. (Originally published in 1869).

Gardner, John W. *Excellence: Can We Be Equal and Excellent Too?* New York: Harper & Row, 1961.

Gartner, Alan, Mary Conway Kohler, and Frank Riessman. *Children Teach Children.* New York: Harper & Row, 1971.

Gerard, R. W., ed. *Computers and Education.* New York: McGraw-Hill, 1967.

Glasser, William. *Schools without Failure.* New York: Harper & Row, 1969.

Goertzel, Victor and Mildred. *Cradles of Eminence.* Boston: Little, Brown, 1962.

Gowan, John Curtis and Catherine B. Bruch. *The Academically Talented and Guidance.* Boston: Houghton-Mifflin, 1971.

Gowan, John Curtis and George D. Demos. *The Education and Guidance of the Ablest.* Springfield, Ill.: Charles C Thomas, 1964.

Gowan, John Curtis and E. Paul Torrance. *Educating the Ablest.* Itasco, Ill.: W. F. Peacock, 1971. (A Book of Readings including original material also.)

Grost, Audrey. *Genius in Residence.* Englewood Cliffs, N. J.: Prentice-Hall, 1970.

Guide To Simulation Games for Education and Training, The. Information Resources, Inc., 1675 Massachusetts Avenue, Cambridge, Mass. 02138.

Guilford, J. P. *Intelligence and Creativity: Their Educational Implications.* San Diego, Calif.: R. Knapp, 1969.

———. *The Nature of Human Intelligence.* New York: McGraw-Hill, 1967.

Hawes, Gene R. *Educational Testing for the Millions, What Tests Really Mean for Your Child.* New York: McGraw-Hill, 1964.

Hermanson, David P. and David C. Wright. *Perceptual Change of Student and Staff toward Learning by Participation in a Seminar Program for the Gifted Learner.* A dissertation presented to the Faculty of the Graduate School of Leadership and Human Behavior, United States International University, and printed by the San Diego City Schools, San Diego, California, June 1969.

Hermanson, David P. and Cecil Munsey. A series of helpful *Working Papers* issued regularly by the San Diego City Schools Secondary Gifted Programs, 1971–1972. Examples: *Individualizing Education for Gifted Senior High School Students; Goals and Objectives for the Secondary Gifted Program 1971–1972* (an Ideabook with 108 practical low-cost objectives); *A Conceptual Framework for a High School for Gifted Students;* and *Dimensions of a Secondary Gifted Program.*

Herndon, James. *The Way It Spozed To Be.* New York: Simon & Schuster, 1968.

Highet, Gilbert. *The Art of Teaching.* New York: Alfred A. Knopf, 1969.

Hill, Mary Broderick. *Enrichment Programs for Intellectually Gifted Pupils.* California Project Talent. Sacramento: California State Department of Education, 1969.

Hollingworth, Leta. *Children Above 180 IQ.* New York: World Book Co., 1942.

Holt, John. *How Children Fail.* New York: Pitman, 1964.

———. *How Children Learn.* New York: Pitman, 1967.

———. *The Underachieving School.* New York: Pitman, 1969.

———. *What Do I Do Monday?* New York: E. P. Dutton, 1970.

Howard, Alvin W. and George C. Stoumbis. *The Junior High and Middle Schools.* Scranton, Pa.: International Textbook, 1970.

Innovation in Education: New Directions for the American School. Committee for Economic Development, 1968.

Kaufman, Bel. *Up the Down Staircase.* Englewood Cliffs, N. J.: Prentice-Hall, 1964.

Kohl, Herbert. *36 Children.* New York: New American Library, 1967.

Kozol, Jonathan. *Death At An Early Age.* Boston: Houghton-Mifflin, 1967.

Lecomte du Noüy, Pierre. *Human Destiny.* New York: Longmans Green, 1947.

Leonard, George. *Education and Ecstasy.* New York: Delacorte Press, 1968.

Marland, Sidney P., Jr. *Education of the Gifted and Talented.* Report to the Congress of the United States by the U. S. Commissioner of Education. Washington, D. C.: Department of Health, Education and Welfare, 1971. 2 vols.

Martinson, Ruth A. *Curriculum Enrichment for the Gifted in Primary Grades.* Englewood Cliffs, N. J.: Prentice-Hall, 1968.

———. See also (under Marland) *Education of the Gifted and Talented, Vol. II,* for her excellent research summary of the field of gifted education.

Montessori, Maria. *The Montessori Method.* New York: Schocken Books, 1964 (first published in English, 1912).

———. *Dr. Montessori's Own Handbook.* New York: Schocken Books, 1965 (first pub. 1914).

———. *Spontaneous Activity in Education.* New York: Schocken Books, 1965 (first pub. 1917).

Petrequin, Gaynor. *Individualizing Learning through Modular-Flexible Programming.* New York: McGraw-Hill, 1968.

Piaget, Jean. *The Psychology of Intelligence.* Totowa, N. J.: Little-field, Adams, 1960.

————. *Science of Education and the Psychology of the Child,* translated from the French by Derek Coltman. New York: Grossman Publishers, 1970; Paris: *Editions Noel,* 1969.

Piltz, Albert, and Robert Sund. *Creative Teaching of Science in the Elementary School.* Boston: Allyn & Bacon, 1968.

Pines, Maya. *Revolution in Learning.* New York: Harper & Row, 1966.

Plowman, Paul D. and Joseph P. Rice. *Final Report: California Project Talent,* Publication No. VI. Sacramento: California State Department of Education, 1969.

Postman, Neil, and Charles Weingartner. *Teaching as a Subversive Activity.* New York: Delacorte Press, 1969.

————. *The Soft Revolution.* New York: Delacorte Press, 1971.

Rice, Joseph P. *The Gifted, Developing Total Talent.* Springfield, Ill.: Charles C Thomas, 1970.

Riessman, Frank and Hermine I. Popper. *Up from Poverty.* New York: Harper & Row, 1968.

Robb, Mel H. *Teacher Assistants, a Blueprint for a Successful Volunteer-Aide Program.* Columbus, Ohio: Charles E. Merrill, 1969.

Rosenthal, Robert, and Lenore Jacobson. *Pygmalion in the Classroom.* New York: Holt, Rinehart and Winston, 1968.

Russell, Bertrand. *Education and the Good Life.* New York: Liveright, 1926. Copyright ® 1954 by Bertrand Russell.

Sanderlin, Owenita. *Creative Teaching.* New York: A. S. Barnes, 1971.

————. *Johnny.* New York: A. S. Barnes, 1968.

Sharp, Evelyn. *Thinking Is Child's Play.* New York: E. P. Dutton, 1969.

Silberman, Charles E. *Crisis in the Classroom.* New York: Random House, 1970.

Strang, Ruth M. *Helping Your Gifted Child.* New York: E. P. Dutton, 1960.

Sumption, Merle E. *Three Hundred Gifted Children.* Yonkers on Hudson, New York: World Book Co., 1941.

Terman, Lewis M., *et al. Genetic Studies of Genius.* Vol. I, *Mental and Physical Traits of a Thousand Gifted Children,* 1926; Vol. II, *The Early Mental Traits of Three Hundred Geniuses,*

1926; Vol. III, *The Promise of Youth, Follow-Up Studies of a Thousand Gifted Children,* 1930; Vol. IV (with Melita Oden), *The Gifted Child Grows Up,* 1947; Vol. V (with Melita Oden), *The Gifted Group at Mid-Life, 35 Years Follow-Up of a Superior Group,* 1959. Stanford, Ca.: Stanford University Press.

Thomas, George, and Joseph Crescimbeni. *Guiding the Gifted Child.* New York: Random House, 1966.

Torrance, E. Paul. *Gifted Children in the Classroom.* New York: Macmillan, 1965.

————. *Guiding Creative Talent,* Englewood Cliffs, N. J.: Prentice-Hall, 1962.

————, ed. *Talent and Education.* Minneapolis, Minn.: University of Minnesota Press, 1960.

————. *Torrance Tests of Creative Thinking.* Princeton, N. J.: Personnel Press, 1966.

Ward, Virgil. *Educating the Gifted: An Axiomatic Approach.* Columbus, Ohio: Charles E. Merrill, 1961.

Weber, Lillian. *The English Infant School and Informal Education.* Englewood Cliffs, N. J.: Prentice-Hall, 1971.

Weinstein, Gerald, and Mario D. Fantini, eds. *Toward Humanistic Education, a Curriculum of Affect.* New York: Praeger, 1970.

White House Conference on Child Health and Protection. *Special Education—the Handicapped and the Gifted, Report of the Committee on Special Classes,* Charles Scott Berry, Chairman. New York: Century Company, 1930. (Interesting to compare to 1971 Report to Congress, *Education of the Gifted and Talented.*)

Witty, Paul, ed. *The Gifted Child.* American Association for Gifted Children. Boston, Mass.: D. C. Heath, 1951.

Wright, Betty Atwell. *Teacher Aides to the Rescue.* New York: John Day, 1969.

Magazine Articles, Speeches, etc.

Asbell, Bernard. "Helping Children to Grow Up Smart." *Redbook,* July 1970.

Bish, Charles, ed. "What's New in Education for the Gifted?" In

Accent on Talent, Vol. II, Washington, D. C.: National Education Association, 1968.

DeMott, Benjamin. Review of Herndon's *How to Survive in Our Native Land. Saturday Review,* September 18, 1971.

Glatthorn, Allan J. and J. F. Ferderbar. "Independent Study—for *All* Students," *Phi Delta Kappan,* March 1966.

Gold, Marvin. "Kentucky's Lincoln School for Disadvantaged Gifted Youngsters." In Gowan and Torrance, *Educating the Ablest,* 1971.

Goodlad, John I. "Meeting Children Where They Are." *Saturday Review,* March 20, 1965.

———. "The Schools *vs.* Education," *Saturday Review,* April 19, 1969.

Gowan, John C. and Catherine Bruch. "What Makes a Creative Person a Creative Teacher?" *The Gifted Child Quarterly* 11, 1967.

Hartshorn, W. C., "Musical Education of the Gifted," *Music Educator's Journal,* February 1968.

Hatch, Albert L. "The HISC, Hatch Interpretive Score of Creativity." Copy may be obtained from Al Hatch, Los Angeles City Schools, Zone D, Los Angeles, California.

Herrnstein, Richard. "IQ." *Atlantic Monthly,* September 1971.

Hersey, John. "Connecticut's Committee for the Gifted," *Educational Leadership,* January 1956.

Honzik, Marjorie P., Jean W. McFarlene and Lucile Allen. "The Stability of Mental Test Performance Between Two and Eighteen Years." *The Journal of Experimental Psychology* 17 (1948).

Illich, Ivan. "The Alternative to Schooling." *Saturday Review,* June 19, 1971.

Isaacs, Ann. "A Survey of Suggested Preparation of Teachers of the Gifted." *The Gifted Child Quarterly* 10, 1966.

Javits, Jacob (Senator). In the *Congressional Record,* January 28, 1969.

Jencks, Christopher. "Intelligence and Race." *The New Republic,* September 13, 1969.

Jensen, Arthur R., "How much can we boost IQ and scholastic achievement?" *Harvard Educational Review* 39 (Winter 1969): 1–123.

Martinson, Ruth, David Hermanson and George Banks. "An Independent Study-Seminar Program for the Gifted." *Exceptional Children,* January 1972.

McLuhan, Marshall. "Electronics and the Psychic Dropout." In *This Book Is About Schools* (a compilation of articles from *This Magazine Is About Schools*). New York: Random House, 1970.

McPartland, James. "Should We Give Up on School Desegregation?" *The Johns Hopkins Magazine,* April 1970.

Meeker, Mary N. "Identifying Potential Giftedness," NASSP *Bulletin,* December 1971.

Mirman, Norman. "Teacher Qualifications for Educating the Gifted." *The Gifted Child Quarterly,* 8, 1964.

Munsey, Cecil. "Some Don't Have 'Em." *Programs for the Gifted Bulletin,* San Diego City Schools, San Diego, California, Spring 1971.

Renzulli, Joseph S. "Designing an Instrument for Evaluating Programs of Differential Education for the Gifted." In *The Gifted: CEC Selected Convention Papers;* Washington, D. C.: Council for Exceptional Children, National Education Association, 1967.

Riessman, Frank. In "What's New in Education for the Gifted?" See Bish, Charles, 1968.

Sanderlin, Owenita. "The Wonderful Age of Four." *Parents' Magazine,* December 1958.

Spock, Benjamin. "Why I Don't Believe in Speeding Up Primary Education." *Redbook,* October 1965.

Steele, Joe M. "Dimensions of the Class Activities Questionnaire." Urbana, Illinois, October 1969. (A pamphlet: address in text.)

Torrance, E. Paul. "Creativity and its Educational Implications for the Gifted." *The Gifted Child Quarterly* 12, 1968.

————. In "What's New in Education for the Gifted?" See Bish, Charles, 1968.

Trump, J. Lloyd and William Georgiades. "Doing Better with What You Have." A pamphlet reprinted from *The Bulletin of the NASSP,* May 1970.

Tunney, John V. (Senator). "How Smart Do You Want Your Child To Be?" *McCall's,* October 1970.

Whitmire, Janet. "The Independent Study Program at Melbourne High." *Phi Delta Kappan,* September 1965.

Witty, Paul, "Intra-Race Testing and Negro Intelligence," *Journal of Psychology* 1 (1936): 179–192.

Zaslow, E. M. "Talent in the Ghetto." *American Education,* March 1967.

Bibliographies

Gowan, J. C. *Annotated Bibliography on the Academically Talented.* Washington, D. C.: National Education Association, 1961.

———. *Annotated Bibliography on Creativity and Giftedness.* Northridge, California: San Fernando Valley State College Foundation, 1965.

Goldberg, I. Ignacy. *Selected Bibliography of Special Education.* New York: Teacher's College, Columbia University, 1967. (Section on gifted books and articles is on pages 75 to 80.)

Gifted and Creativity Programs: A Selective Bibliography, February 1971 and *Gifted and Creativity Research: A Selective Bibliography,* February 1971. These annotated bibliographies are available without charge from the Information Center on Exceptional Children, the Council for Exceptional Children, Jefferson Plaza, Suite 900, 1411 South Jefferson Davis Highway, Arlington, Virginia 22202.

Specialty Journals

The National Elementary Principal. The February 1972 issue is an outstanding one, specializing in the education of the gifted and talented. It contains much up-to-date information.

The Gifted Child Quarterly. Published by the National Association for Gifted Children, 8080 Springvalley Road, Cincinnati, Ohio 45326. Ann Isaacs, Editor.

The Journal of Creative Behavior. Bishop Hall, SUNY, 1300 Elmwood Ave., Buffalo, New York 14222. Dr. Sidney Parnes, Director.

Educational Facilities Laboratory Reports
(of special interest)

For free copy write 477 Madison Avenue, New York, N. Y. 10022.

Educational Change and Architectural Consequences, by Ronald Gross and Judith Murphy, with educational advice of Dr. Robert Finley and Dr. Thomas Hasenpflug, directed by architect Ronald W. Haase, AIA, 1968.

Middle Schools, by Judith Murphy, 1965.

The School Library, Facilities for Independent Study in the Secondary School by Ralph E. Ellsworth and Hobart D. Wagener, 1963.

School Scheduling by Computer, The Story of GASP, by Judith Murphy, 1964.

Schools Without Walls, 1965.

Films

Bailey Films, Inc., 6509 DeLongpre Ave., Hollywood, California.
"Operation Head Start," 16 minutes, b. & w.
"Rafe: Developing Giftedness in the Educationally Disadvantaged." 20 minutes, color.

International Film Bureau, 332 South Michigan Ave., Chicago, Ill.
"Who Is Pete?" Use of all kinds of tests, sixth grade student.

McGraw-Hill, New York, N. Y.
"Challenge of the Gifted." 12 minutes, color.
"Portrait of the Inner City School: A Place to Learn."

Sterling Movies, Inc. Chicago, Ill.
"And No Bells Ring." 56 minutes, b. & w., reorganization of the secondary school, reviews the Trump Report. See J. Lloyd Trump.

Miscellaneous

RIF—Reading Is Fun-damental: Margaret McNamara's give-a-book program for motivation of the disadvantaged. Smithsonian Institute, Washington, D. C. 20560, will send information.

"Where the Money Is," a very clear guide to available federal funds published in *American Education* annually, and distributed as a reprint from Supt. of Documents, U. S. Government Printing Office, Washington, D. C. 20402. 20¢ per copy.

Gifted Organizations

American Association for the Gifted, 15 Gramercy Park, New York, N. Y. 10003. Pauline Williamson, Executive Director.

The Association for the Gifted (TAG), a division of The Council for Exceptional Children, 1411 South Jefferson Davis Highway, Arlington, Virginia 22202. John Curtis Gowan, President.

Council of State Directors of Programs for Gifted, California State Department of Education, 721 Capital Mall, Sacramento, California 95814. Paul D. Plowman, President.

National Association for Gifted Children (NAG), 8080 Springvalley Drive, Cincinnati, Ohio 45236. Ann Isaacs, Executive Director.

U. S. Office of Education, Office of Gifted and Talented Education, Room 2100, ROB-3, 7th and D Streets, S.W., Washington, D. C. 20202. Director, Harold Lyon; Deputy Director Jane Case Williams.

The Steering Committee of the National Coordinating Council for the Education of the Gifted and Talented. For information write Dr. Virginia Ehrlich, Gifted Child Studies Dept., Bureau of Educational Research, NYC Board of Education, 40 Seventh Ave., New York, N. Y. 10014.

England: The National Association for Gifted Children, 27 John Adam Street, London, W. C. 2, England. Miss Camilla Ruegg, Executive Secretary.

Your State Education Agency, located in the capital of your state, or your local school district, may be able to furnish information on state and local organizations for teachers, parents and other interested groups. Find out and write in below any such names or addresses. If necessary, start one!

Index

179